Bertrand Russell

BERTRAND RUSSELL

HERBERT GOTTSCHALK

Bertrand Russell: a Life

Translated from the German by
EDWARD FITZGERALD

ROY PUBLISHERS INC.
NEW YORK

English translation
by Edward Fitzgerald
© *1965*
John Baker Publishers Limited
from the original German
'Bertrand Russell eine Biographie' von Herbert Gottschalk
© *1962*
Colloquium Verlag Otto H. Hess,
Berlin 45

Library of Congress No. 66-10773

7584

Printed in Great Britain by
Northumberland Press Limited
Gateshead

Contents

1 Introduction

HARDLY any philosopher has been as well known during his lifetime as Bertrand Russell, though this is due less to his philosophic labours than to his constant preoccupation with the tremendous world-wide questions that concern our generation. The older Russell grew, the better known his name became – which means that most people have never known him as anything but a small gentleman with a fine head of whitish hair, a prominent nose and sardonic mouth, and a lively ironic smile. He was born in an era which already belongs to history, and he assimilated the ideas of the nineteenth century and he approved of its devotion to human progress. Though in the meantime two world wars have shaken belief in the essential reasonableness of mankind Bertrand Russell still stands firm. Unshakeably convinced that the free man must fight to the end for the preservation of his freedom, he is always to be found in the front ranks of those who want to save peace in a threatened world. In consequence at the age of almost ninety he once again suffered arrest for defying authority.

In 1937 he wrote his own obituary, and it was published in *The Times* and other newspapers on June 1st, 1962, shortly before his ninetieth birthday. He describes himself in this auto-obituary as a man of unusual principles, but one who at least is always prepared to live up to them.

Following unwittingly in the footsteps of Frege he established his scientific reputation at the beginning of the present century by the publication of *Principia Mathematica*, a work he wrote in conjunction with Alfred Whitehead. Breaking with traditional philosophic thought he sought to make mathematical logic the basis of philosophy, though since then doubts are beginning to arise concerning the validity of this undertaking. The thesis is disputed, for example, by Professor Freytag-Löringhoff, and by Professor Günther Jacoby.

Nevertheless, Russell's own performance remains undiminished. He was never interested in building up a rigid philosophic system but in serving scientific truth to the best of his ability in his own way. Because of this he has never found it difficult to admit errors once he has recognized them, or to turn freely to newly-won truths. This has more than once brought a reproach that he lacks consistency – and even firmness of character.

The turbulent affairs of the world finally swept him out of his scholarly seclusion, and he publicly denounced the basis of what he regarded as an out-of-date morality which constantly led to new wars. In a great number of popularly written publications he put forward constructive proposals for reforms in all spheres of life. People were shocked and scandalized by his frankness, a quality which is characteristic of the man, and although it can hardly be said to have changed the world as a whole it has nevertheless stimulated the minds of many people.

Bertrand Russell's published works fill a quite impressive shelf and amount to something like seventy volumes. They include his many important lectures, but not his innumerable reviews, newspaper articles and wireless and television talks. The world-wide interest he arouses is due to some extent to his wit and eloquence and to his brilliant gift of presenting difficult problems in an entertaining and understandable fashion.

2 Family, Childhood and Youth

IF YOU trace back Bertrand Russell's family tree you will be forced to the somewhat trite conclusion that as the bough bends so the twig inclines. Burke's *Peerage* provides us with interesting details concerning the forefathers of our philosopher. It is not surprising to find that there were some outstanding personalities among them, men who were notable both for their eccentricity and their moral courage, men who were frequently the centre of vehement dispute and controversy.

One of the favourite courtiers of Henry VIII, a certain John Russell, was rewarded for his services with Woburn Abbey, which subsequently became the seat of the family he founded. The process of sequestration was carried out with great simplicity: the abbot was hanged from a convenient oak tree, and his monks were driven out. This royal gift was handed down from generation to generation of Russells, and is at present in the possession of the thirteenth Duke of Bedford, a kinsman of Bertrand Russell.

The first Earl of Bedford, John Russell, was a rich man who owned a number of estates scattered around over the country, including Covent Garden and Bloomsbury. The fourth Earl of Bedford made something of a name for himself by draining a good deal of low-lying land in Yorkshire. The Bedfords now received the ducal title from William of Orange, who conferred it on the fifth earl as some compensation for the fact that one of his sons had been executed for high treason under the Stuarts.

Lord John Russell, Bertrand Russell's grandfather, was born as the third son of the sixth Duke of Bedford, and during the long reign of Queen Victoria he was twice Prime Minister. Bertrand Russell can just re-member him as a very old and physically feeble man who was occasionally wheeled out into the sunshine in a bath chair, was always amiably disposed to his grand-children and put up with their racket patiently.

In his second marriage he took the daughter of the Earl of Minto as wife, and her eldest son received the title of Lord Amberley. He married Kate, the daughter of Lord Stanley, and she bore him three children. The first son was born in 1868. This was Frank, who on the death of his grandfather became the second Lord Rus-sell. In 1868, the second child, Rachel, the only daugh-ter, was born, and the youngest and last child, Bertrand, was born on May 18th, 1872.

The doctor who was present at Bertrand's birth announced approvingly that the boy was a fine baby. At first his mother found him somewhat ugly, but well cared for, he grew up healthily and happily. How-ever, when the boy could just about stand on his own feet, his father began to suffer from epileptic fits, and a little later his brother, Bertrand's uncle, lost his reason. Bertrand was two years old when first his brother and then his sister, and finally his mother, who was looking after the youngest herself, went down with diphtheria. The elder boy, Frank, was a tough child and he soon recovered, but the sister, Rachel, and the mother both died. Lord Amberley survived this double blow only about eighteen months, and then the two brothers were orphans.

Before he died Lord Amberley appointed tutors for his two sons so that they should be brought up in accordance with his own liberal and free-thinking outlook. But these arrangements were not carried out and the Court of Chancery directed that the two children should go to live with their paternal grandparents at Pembroke Lodge, a fine house at Richmond given by Queen Victoria to her loyal statesman Lord John Russell, as a place in which to spend his declining years.

In 1946 *The Philosophy of Bertrand Russell*, Volume V of the Library of Living Philosophers, was published in America. In addition to essays expounding and criticizing his philosophical views by twenty-one of his eminent contemporaries, this volume contained a short autobiography by Russell, entitled 'My Mental Development'. This was subsequently republished as part of his 'Autobiography'. He tells us how as a small child he went to live in the house of his grandparents, and that as he heard little or nothing about his dead parents whilst he was there he gradually began to suspect the existence of some dark secret, so puzzling was the veil of silence. He was twenty-one before the veil was lifted, and it was then that he obtained access to documents which he subsequently edited and published under the title of *The Amberley*

Papers. It was from these documents that he learned that his father had gone through very much the same intellectual and emotional development as himself.

It was expected of Lord Amberley that in accordance with the family tradition of public service he would go in for politics, and, indeed, for a short period, from 1867 to 1868, he was actually a member of parliament. But neither by temperament nor conviction was he the stuff of which successful politicians are made. For one thing, in his youth he had rejected Christianity and become a follower of the empiricist John Stuart Mill, whose ideas Bertrand also enthusiastically embraced as a young man. Both Lord Amberley and his wife were enthusiastic supporters of Mill's ideas, and particularly his advocacy of votes for women and birth control. Such ideas meant that the noble Lord was subjected to a barrage of opposition from the Church and public opinion, and he went down to defeat. Bertrand Russell recalls a somewhat similar situation in which he found himself in the United States in the early forties because of his unconventional beliefs in the matter of marital morality. Lord Amberley sought to secure his return to parliament, but he did not succeed. In the meantime he wrote a voluminous book entitled *Analysis of Religious Belief,* which was published posthumously. His son subsequently declared that a political career was in any case quite hopeless where his father was concerned because of his readiness to admit his weak points, at the same time drawing attention to the strong points of his opponents. In addition he was hampered by physical fraility and ill health. Lady Amberley loyally supported her husband's views and was a supporter of women's suffrage.

Bertrand Russell's grandfather died in 1878, shortly after his grandsons had moved into his house. After his death his widow, Bertrand's still vigorous grandmother, supervised the boys' education. Although Bertrand generally disagreed with her views he nevertheless admits that she had a great influence on his development. She came of a Scottish Presbyterian family and she retained her somewhat puritanical mode of life to the end. She despised comfort, attached no very great importance to food, and rejected wine and tobacco. She stood fast by these principles although, until her husband retired from active politics, she had moved in the fashionable world of her class. Bertrand recalls that the family and the servants assembled every morning at eight o'clock for prayers. Although eight servants were kept, the table was of spartan simplicity, and if ever anything a little more tasty came to the table, such as an apple tart, it was there just to be looked at as far as the children were concerned, and they had to content themselves with their rice pudding. Wine was served, but only when guests were present, and only for them. Cold baths were the order of the day throughout the year. And every day before breakfast Bertrand had to practise his scales for half an hour at the piano. The only value was virtue, and this was confidently expected to lead everybody to wisdom, health and happiness. Mathematics and philosophy, two subjects in which Bertrand soon became interested, were on the proscribed list – particularly mathematics, because it had no ethical content.

Grandmother was anxious to guide the two boys along the right path to a useful and vigorous life. She was not interested in any other way of arriving at success, and 'good matches' had no place in her plans. The Protestant idea of personal responsibility towards God was her guiding light. Bertrand Russell still has the Bible she presented to him on his twelfth birthday. In it is a dedication in her own hand exhorting him for the future conduct of his life to abjure the crowd and do no evil, to fear not and be of good cheer – advice which he was to follow unswervingly throughout his life, even long after he had broken with Christianity, from whose philosophy the maxims were culled by his grandmother.

At the age of seventy, finding that she was, after all, unable to stomach the doctrine of the Holy Trinity, the old lady turned her back on the Presbyterians and joined the Unitarians. Her religious faith and her puritanical rule of life did not prevent her from taking a very lively interest in political affairs. She was in favour of Home Rule for Ireland, and she shocked her friends and acquaintances by establishing friendly personal relationships with certain Irish members of parliament who were supposed to have connived at political assassination. She condemned British imperialism and she opposed all wars whose object was the subjugation of 'primitive' peoples.

As France was still suspect, from the days of Napoleon, of dictatorial and autocratic leanings, Bertrand and his elder brother Frank had Swiss and German governesses, and they both learned German as their first foreign tongue. Frank was a gay and lively child, even somewhat wild, whereas Bertrand was reserved and rather shy, qualities which caused him to be regarded as a well-behaved child. In fact, during a visit of Queen Victoria to the house, he earned high praise for his model behaviour. Frank, on the other hand, so disliked the discipline of his grandmother's house that he ran away, and when he returned he threatened to run away again unless he was sent to boarding school. He had his way. Bertrand remained the obedient child at home and went regularly to church where he learned the hymns so diligently that even now he still knows many of them by heart. His favourite occupation was going for long walks in the great park and allowing his thinking free rein. He dug deep holes in the ground and came to the conclusion that the world could not be round, since otherwise he would have emerged in Australia. The stories adults told him about angels were soon dismissed. These childish assertions increasingly strengthened his desire to get at the core of things and find out the truth about them. He adopted a certain scepticism towards everything other people told him. No wonder that mathematics attracted him even when he was quite young, because he hoped that this world of figures would help him to get at the truth. When his brother attempted to teach him Euclid's geometry he wanted to know why mathematics had to operate with axioms. In this way he became interested in the principle of mathematics from his very earliest years.

But in his grandmother's house there was something that particularly fascinated him, and this was his grandfather's library. In his delvings he came across a mass of old historical books and this aroused his interest in history. The library had become his own study since the death of his grandfather, and he browsed among the old volumes. In particular Bertrand admired his forebear Lord William Russell, who was executed in the reign of Charles II. The example of this noble ancestor convinced Bertrand that resistence to properly constituted authority was sometimes right and proper if not always profitable.

He was less enthusiastic for Gibbon and Swift than for Shelley, but one way and another he provided himself with a fairly catholic literary education. In fact he read so much that at the age of sixteen it almost cost him his eyesight. It was at about this time that he began to concern himself with questions of religion, and to think about the problems of free-will, immortality and God. This interest was encouraged by his free-thinking tutor, but the man was dismissed because it was rightly feared that his influence was undermining the faith of the growing boy. This was locking the stable door after the horse had bolted; the seeds of doubt had already been sown. Bertrand confided his thoughts to a diary, using the Greek alphabet for the purpose. In this not particularly happy time of growth and development he did his best not to allow his ideas to be influenced by his desires. It was now that he first began to doubt free-will, and then immortality. His reading of the autobiography of John Stuart Mill completed the process and led to the final rejection of the idea of God and to the adoption of the principle that only what was proved by experience should be accepted as truth. Such ideas could naturally not be expressed openly in the house of his grandmother. The only thing he did not take over from Mill was the latter's assertion that all mathematical generalizations had developed from experience. This encouraged him to penetrate still more deeply into the fundamentals of mathematics.

Bertrand's grandmother did not like public schools, so that when her grandchild expressed a determined wish to go to Cambridge a private tutor was engaged to teach him sufficient Latin and Greek to get him through the preliminary examination. Because he had to make up for his lack of classical knowledge in the space of eighteen months he never attained the degree of fluency in the classical tongues that he already possessed in a number of modern ones. German, Italian and French never presented any difficulties, particularly as it was the custom at Pembroke Lodge to talk with foreign guests in their own languages.

Bertrand's grandmother did not long oppose his wish to go to Cambridge, but she insisted that he should prepare himself so thoroughly that he could win a scholarship. There was no shortage of money in the family, of course, and Bertrand's stay at Cambridge raised no financial problems. The insistence that he should win an exhibition scholarship was a disciplinary measure.

Bertrand's entrance examination for Trinity College was supervised by Alfred Whitehead, who at once recognized the young man's talent and helped him to establish his first friendships at Cambridge. It was only now in the freer air of the university that Russell realized that he had been living in an atmosphere which tended to inhibit thought. In Cambridge he could breathe freely for the first time and talk naturally as among equals without immediately being condemned as either mad or bad. It was a tremendous pleasure for him to live in a world in which Reason was regarded as a goddess and a keen intellect as a virtue. In his very first term he made life-long friends. It has been said that as a child he did not miss contact and intercourse with young people of his own age, but looking back Russell frankly admits that the loneliness of his early years was often a heavy burden, and he adds that from the beginning at Cambridge he never lacked friends.

He still recalls those first friends very clearly. First of all there was the conservative Hegelian McTaggart, and then Lowes Dickinson, a classical philologist, whom everyone held in great regard because of his own amiable nature. Other friends were the two brothers Crompton and Theodor Llewelyn Davies, the son of the clergyman who translated Plato's *Republic*. Russell records that they were all men unusually open to friendship, and, like him, they were all moved by the desire to do something good and useful in the world. A few years later the younger Crompton was just at the beginning of what would certainly have been a distinguished Civil Service career when he was drowned while bathing. For a short while Russell shared rooms with Charles Sanger, who subsequently became a prominent lawyer, a keen mathematician and a linguist. The three brothers Trevelyan were also amongst his close friends at Cambridge. Charles, the eldest, subsequently played a prominent role in the

Labour Party, which he finally left because he felt that it wasn't Socialist enough. Robert Trevelyan became known as a poet and translator, and George was the well-known historian. G. E. Moore was rather younger than Bertrand Russell, but his philosophic views were not without effect on Russell's own work.

This close association with good friends thawed out Russell's original shyness and he soon began to talk in that frank and trenchant fashion which was subsequently responsible for a great deal of his popularity. His main subject was mathematics, which he studied zealously, but the discussions among his friends also concerned philosophy, history and other sciences. Russell now joined an undergraduates' association known as 'The Society', or 'The Apostles'. Its members met at the week-ends, and their discussions often went on all night. After breakfast on Sunday mornings they would wander out into the countryside and remain there the rest of the day, mulling over their problems.

Bertrand Russell enjoyed these discussions as one of the great gifts of his freedom. The opportunity to exchange thoughts, and to express freely the things which were moving him, was an important, indeed, essential corollary to his own private studies. This was true at Cambridge and it remained true throughout the whole of his long life. His study of mathematics was not giving him quite the satisfaction he had hoped, and he was less interested in pure mathematics than in the philosophy of mathematics. The orthodox ideas expressed by his tutors proved unacceptable to him, and he felt that their beliefs contained errors and fallacies. On the other hand he could find no satisfactory answers to the burning questions that engaged him. At the end of three years his disappointment caused him to sell his mathematical text-books and transfer his attention to philosophy.

There is no doubt that in those days Cambridge had a clear advantage over Oxford in the sphere of the natural sciences, and in the subsequent years it could proudly list the names of many great men, including Whitehead, Ramsay, Keynes, Wittgenstein, Moore, Rutherford and W. E. Johnson. Cambridge provided Bertrand Russell with the ideal basis of a philosophy associated with the natural sciences. Under the influence of McTaggart he first occupied himself intensively with Hegelian philosophy, allowing himself to be persuaded that Hegel and Kant were far ahead of Locke, Hume and Berkeley in their philosophical thought, and that even the much-admired John Stuart Mill could not hold his ground with them. Russell's tutor Stout strengthened this preference for Hegel, and drew his attention to F. H. Bradley's book *Appearance and Reality,* which caused a great stir when it was first published in 1893. Because of the contradictions to be found in it, Bradley relegated the world of everyday life to the realm of appearances and postulated the Absolute, 'the infinite coherent unity', as the only reality. All things existed only in the idea of the Absolute. At this stage of his life Bertrand Russell's admiration for Bradley was almost boundless, but inwardly he was nevertheless dissatisfied to find that his philosophical thought was becoming so far removed from empiricism that his own main interest, the foundations of mathematics, was being pushed into the background again.

He went down in 1894. It was a period in which optimism with regard to the future was the general feeling. Young men looked back at the creative achievements of the nineteenth century and felt an ardent desire to serve the cause of progress and take their part in building 'the golden future'. This belief in human progress was so strong that wars between civilized peoples were no longer regarded as practical politics; they were a buried error of man's past. While he was still at Cambridge, Bertrand Russell wrote that, quite apart from politics, certain traditional moral ideas must now give way to more modern views, since a world which was developing to something higher and better could not possibly allow itself to be shackled by an outworn system of ethics. However, no doubt under the influence of a puritanical upbringing which had not yet entirely lost its hold on him, these ideas were only very moderately and tentatively expressed.

Although Bertrand Russell's shyness gradually began to be dissipated in intellectual matters it remained crippling where young women were concerned. He had little or no association with them, so that when he now fell in love with Alys Pearsall Smith, the daughter of a Quaker family, he proved a rather taciturn and embarrassed suitor, though at the same time a most determined and persistent one. His grandmother naturally regarded the match as unsuitable and insisted at least on a probation period, so Bertrand was banished to Paris as attaché to the British Ambassador in the hope that the appointment, and in particular life in the French capital, would turn his thoughts away from marriage. In fact, he found his diplomatic functions boring and his desire for Alys undiminished. Once again he had his way: he abandoned the beginnings of a diplomatic career at the early age of twenty-two, and returned to England in 1894 to marry Alys, who was five years older. His grandmother regarded his abandonment of a diplomatic and political career almost as an act of treachery towards his ancestors, but, in fact, Bertrand had refused the traditional career of his forefathers because he found himself irresistibly attracted to the study of philosophy. This decision represented the first real family breach and he found it painful.

3 Socialism and Mathematics

THE fact that he had decided to abandon diplomacy and politics as a career certainly did not mean that he was not interested in politics – his attachment to the historical process was too firmly rooted for that. He was deeply interested in the ideas and theories which, so to speak, stood godfather to historical happenings, and particularly in those ideas and theories which had shaped the features of his own age. His convictions naturally carried him into the Liberal camp. There was as yet no Labour Party, and the Liberals and Conservatives shared the field as hostile brothers, but educated people were already beginning to talk about the Fabians.

These were the members of the Fabian Society, founded in 1884 by a group of Socialist intellectuals led by Edward Pease, who was also its secretary for many years. Its aim was to reconstruct society 'in accordance with the highest moral possibilities', and as this was obviously going to be a slow job it took its name from the Roman statesman and general, Fabius Cunctator, since they held that 'the long taking of counsel' would be necessary before they could put their Socialist ideals into practice. It was obvious, therefore, that the Fabians must be firm opponents of Marxism and its revolutionary class-struggle principle. Their aim was to achieve Socialism gradually within the framework of the established political and constitutional order. Like their namesake they stood for slow, gradual and patient progress. Amongst their best-known members were Bernard Shaw, H. G. Wells and Sidney and Beatrice Webb. Bernard Shaw was responsible for *Fabian Essays*, which began to appear in 1893. It was this same year that Keir Hardie founded the Independent Labour Party, with the encouragement and assistance of the Fabians.

Russell now began to interest himself in Socialism, and this naturally caused him to inquire into the economic background of its theory. Shortly after his marriage he went with his wife to Berlin to study the German Socialist movement. Russell's wife was related to the British Ambassador in Berlin and this produced an invitation to dinner at the Embassy. However, the two guests so shocked their hosts by telling them that they had actually attended a Socialist meeting in the city that no further invitations were ever extended.

To tell the truth, Russell and his wife found these Social Democratic meetings rather boring, but they continued to frequent them because despite the monotony there was always something to be learned. In the meantime Russell zealously studied Marx's *Capital*, and he is certainly one of those few who have read it from cover to cover. He also read the *Manifesto of the Communist Party*, which from the literary point of view he regarded as one of the most remarkable political pronouncements in history.

On his return to London Bertrand Russell delivered

a series of lectures on his experiences in Germany to the students of the newly-founded London School of Economics, and to the members of the Fabian Society. The result of his studies then appeared in a more permanent form in his book *German Social Democracy*, published in 1896. Even at that time he seemed to possess an instinctive flair for sensing the main lines of future political developments, and this gift was combined with the ability to deal with 'political dynamite' in a scientific and dispassionate fashion, and to write and speak about such matters coolly and objectively. It was also his great strength as a journalist: everything he wrote was based strictly on the known facts, eschewing both sensationalism and wishful thinking.

Temperamentally he was, of course, profoundly sympathetic to Socialism in its many and varied forms, not excluding even Marxism. He was always on the side of those who were fighting in the name of Socialism against the evils of poverty. The *Manifesto of the Communist Party* of Marx and Engels impressed him particularly because of its dismissal of all conventional values, its contempt for traditional morality and religion, and its clear-eyed lack of all illusions. However, this approval in principle did not prevent his analysing and criticizing Marxism from his more remote standpoint as a British Liberal. He deplored the stodginess of Marx and he exposed certain false conclusions, particularly in the Marxist theory of value. In addition Bertrand Russell was opposed to the idea that the State should take over all a country's industries at one swoop, and he considered that gradual nationalization would be a more sensible tactic. This process could go forward slowly and step by step as one industry after the other reached the monopolist stage and was ripe for taking over. One fact he found altogether incomprehensible was that Marx should have overlooked such a simple and obvious symptom as the rise of the middle class, whose ranks were constantly being replenished from amongst the technicians working in the process of production.

However, Bertrand Russell himself was far more interested in the practical question of the everyday policy to be pursued by Socialists if they were to exercise any tangible influence on affairs rather than in the often abstruse theoretical disputes between them. He felt that solid, practical influence on affairs could not be gained through any high-faluting, head-in-the-clouds aims, and he regarded insistence on anything of the sort as a cardinal error. He felt that the noisier and angrier the shouting the foggier became the aims and the more confused the ideas. Socialists had positively provoked the class struggle by their own unwise behaviour. Their aggressive propaganda was driving all their enemies into one united defence against them. This was a lesson, he assured them, they could easily learn from a study of conditions in Germany, where the great majority of the people still upheld the old values represented by the family, religion and the Fatherland, and regarded Socialism with mistrust. By insisting fanatically on their own dogmas Socialists isolated themselves and made any fruitful co-operation with other progressive groups impossible. He severely criticized this attitude, and he pointed out that far from clearing the way for desirable and well-meaning reforms it positively barred the way. Socialists in particular ought to be in favour of a gradual realization of their ideas for a juster and better world. In particular he condemned intolerance and fanaticism even though he could see that it reinforced the solidarity of the Socialist movement and provided Socialists with a kind of secular substitute for religious beliefs and patriotism. He concluded his observations on German Social Democracy by saying that in his opinion, and as things stood, the German people would sooner suffer economic hardships and bow their necks to a military dictatorship than accept Socialism.

In the meantime, however, his recommendation to the German Social Democrats that they should press reforms patiently and gradually was being carried out in his own country where nascent Labour was working together with the Liberals. When the Labour Party adopted more radical measures between the wars it found itself outmanoeuvred by the Conservatives.

In 1896 the Russells paid a three-months visit to the United States, and Bertrand lectured on mathematics at the Johns Hopkins University and at Bryn Mawr College. This visit was of particular interest to Mrs Russell whose family originally came from Quakers of Philadelphia. Their first personal visit in the United States was to Walt Whitman, whom they both greatly admired. Russell said subsequently that this visit helped to emancipate him from the provincialism which prevailed at Cambridge. Whilst in the United States he became acquainted with the work of the German mathematician Weierstrass, whose theory of analytical functions was to prove of great importance for the development of mathematics—yet whilst he was at Cambridge Bertrand Russell had never even heard the name mentioned.

On their return to England the Russells settled down in a modest house in Sussex, where Bertrand had a large study in which he could devote himself completely to his philosophy as he had enough money to allow him to live modestly without working for a living. In the meantime his wife worked for temperance societies, attended high-minded women's clubs, and saw to it that Bertrand's studies were not interrupted. In the evenings when they were together she would often read aloud to him, usually from historical works. His friends noticed that he was always neatly dressed and that he avoided all excesses, and, in fact, he regarded moderation in living as an absolute condition for the maintenance of good health. In particular he avoided alcohol, believing that abstention helped to keep his mind clear. It was a period of burgeoning ideas for him and he did not want it to be disturbed by sickness. What remained completely unchanged by his marriage was his intellectual objectivity, his irony, and his mistrust of all traditional emotions and conventions.

In 1895, he became a Fellow of his old College, Trinity, and wrote a dissertation on the fundamentals of geometry. This work was much praised by both Ward and Whitehead, and this tipped the balance in favour of his remaining loyal to the study of philosophy. If this effort proved a failure it was his intention to turn to economics.

In 1898 he read Hegel again, and this time he came

to the conclusion that everything the great man had to say about mathematics was 'confused nonsense'.

It was at this time, too, that he began to feel doubts about Bradley's theory of non-relational reality, and, indeed, of the whole logical basis of monism. He found himself supported in this by G. E. Moore, who was also beginning to turn against idealism as a result of the same doubts. Bertrand Russell now returned to the basis of realism, feeling that all things must necessarily be real, and that, in any case, Hegel's 'proofs' of non-existence now seemed to lack all cogency. Later on he was to modify this view to some extent by admitting that although there was no logical reason to describe anything as real there was, on the other hand, no logical reason for doubting its reality.

He felt joyfully that this solution had released him from a prison, and that henceforth he would never find himself in the strait jacket of subjectivism again – grass really was green, and the stars in the firmament were realities and not phantoms. He was delighted to be able to experience space and time as something directly existent again, and his idea that despite the contentions of the Hegelians mathematics must be true after all was given a fresh impetus.

This new line of thought was made very obvious in one or two passages of his book *A Critical Exposition of the Philosophy of Leibniz*, published in 1900. This particular book owes its origin to the chance circumstance that McTaggart wanted to visit his family in New Zealand and asked Bertrand Russell to take over the Leibniz lecture he had undertaken to deliver at Cambridge.

However, this work did not tempt Bertrand Russell
to neglect his main interest: an investigation into the
principles of mathematics. It was at about this time
that he attended the international philosophical congress in Paris, and there he made the acquaintance
of the Italian Peano, whose logical and trenchant contributions to the discussions made a deep impression
on him. Peano presented Bertrand Russell with a copy
of his book on symbolic logic, and on reading it
Bertrand Russell found that its author contended
that mathematics was merely 'a more highly developed
form of logic'. Logic had previously always been regarded as the domain of philosophy, and entirely
reserved to it. It was therefore something of a closed
preserve for mathematicians. Before Bertrand Russell
left to attend this congress the first draft of his book
The Principles of Mathematics was complete, but
thanks to his meeting with Peano his ideas now received
new sustenance. The book was to appear in two volumes, the first of which would confine itself to
popularly understandable explanations, whilst the
second would provide mathematical proof that mathematics and logic were identical. Symbolic logic was a
product of the nineteenth century, and it was developed
by men like G. Peano, C. S. Pierce, E. Schröder and G.
Frege, whose ranks Bertrand Russell now joined.

Alfred Whitehead took a great interest in Russell's
work, and in the end they decided to write *Principia
Mathematica* together. The work on this book lasted
the decade from 1900 to 1910, and at the end of it three
large printed volumes were ready. They co-operated
in the sense that each author dealt with certain aspects

of the problem: Whitehead's interest was chiefly mathematical, Russell's chiefly philosophical. They regularly communicated their results to each other and carried out revision together. The final draft for the press was prepared by Bertrand Russell. It was a laborious undertaking full of traps, and he lighted on contradictions in logic itself whilst he was engaged in it. For example, he checked Cantor's proof of the nonexistence of a maximum cardinal number by the methods of traditional logic, and in examining the so-called 'classes' he came to an ambiguous result, a contretemps he ascribed to the defectiveness of logic itself, and promptly suggested that it should be revised. This proposal was received with a certain amount of mockery amongst the *cognoscenti*, but, in fact, it was not long before other scientists began to regard the problem as a real one.

During the course of his work Bertrand Russell discovered that progress in the desired direction could be made even if the 'classes' were ignored altogether. The available logical apparatus was by no means as complete as Russell and Whitehead had supposed. Whitehead worked out new systems of notation which could be expressed symbolically without having recourse to the vague descriptions of ordinary conversation. Summed up as briefly as possible, the *Principia Mathematica* culminates in the definition of Number 1, and in its second volume it proves that $m \times n = n \times m$.

When they started their work neither Russell nor Whitehead knew that Gottlob Frege was already some way ahead of them, advancing in the same direction. With Peano he now became, so to speak, one of the two

Godfathers of *Principia Mathematica*. Frege was professor of mathematics at Jena University. Some of his work concerned itself with providing proof that arithmetic was a part of logic. In this respect he, too, had come across paradoxical results of the same nature as those that were making Bertrand Russell's work so difficult, and when Russell wrote to him on the point in 1901 he replied: 'Arithmetic has begun to totter'.

What Russell was out to do was to deprive mathematics of its halo – or its cloven foot, whichever way you like to look at it. He wanted to prove that there was no impenetrable and mystic background, or a mysterious No-Man's-Land, that anyone could interpret for himself just as he pleased. He proceeded with scientific objectivity to divest mathematics of its mystery and explain it in such a way that every sensible man could appreciate its simplicity.

From his didactic Olympus and the elevated scientific plane on which his proof moved he could naturally not expect to make any general impact, particularly as mathematics is a book with seven seals even for the great majority of educated men, and probably always will be. But he really was disappointed to find that even people who were engaged professionally on the same material were not reading his book either. In all he came across only six people who claimed to have studied the last part of his book with its mathematical methods. At best the philosophic parts of the book were being read by people anxious to discover whether mathematics was really based on logical principles. And even such readers were few and far between.

Bertrand Russell kept running up against new difficulties in his mathematical philosophy, and now and
again he was on the verge of despair. Then suddenly it
struck him that it might help if he could first solve
the problem of description. He hoped in this way to
develop a useful technique which would bring him
nearer to his objective, so in 1905 he grappled with
the problem of linguistics. He had read what Meinong,
a professor of philosophy at Graz University, had to
say about the evidence concerning non-existent things,
and he found himself in disagreement with the formu-
lations Meinong had chosen, such as 'The golden
mountain does not exist', and 'The round square does
not exist'. Meinong went on to say that there was a
golden mountain, which was a mountain and golden,
but still did not exist. Bertrand Russell did not agree.
In his view what Meinong ought to have said was:
'Nothing exists which is at the same time golden and a
mountain'. Only in this way would there be no reason
to suppose that there must exist an unreal object to
be the entity denoted by the phrase 'golden mountain'.

In 1905, at a time when he was already being talked
about in the international scientific world, Bertrand
Russell wrote an article 'On Denoting' in *Mind*, a
leading philosophical journal. However, the *cognoscenti* hardly knew what to say about the matter until
he returned to it in *Principia Mathematica*. His book
Theory of Descriptions, published in 1905, was an
answer to Meinong, but it went far beyond that and it
proved an immediate success in philosophical circles.

Until now it had occurred to no one that the gram-
matical and logical structures of a sentence were not

the same, and that they could therefore not be identical with each other. According to this therefore words expressed a certain something and received the meaning they expressed. Therefore the golden mountain referred to by Meinong must actually exist. Bertrand Russell now analysed this sentence about the golden mountain, and adduced proof that the assumption was incorrect, since by words and semantic relationships one could arrive at thoroughly false conclusions. He reinforced his assertion with numerous other examples. His doubt was based on the hypothesis that a word need not in each case have a fixed and never-changing meaning.

Almost everything we learn is conveyed to us in words. If the words are wrongly used in any way then the sense they are intended to express can become completely distorted, and in consequence we shall receive a wrong picture of the world. Thus the harmony between thought and being depends on the correct use of words.

The layman may well feel that such involved ratiocination is ridiculous, and it may even make him doubt whether a science which concerns itself with such hair-splitting has any right to exist at all. He does not realize that it can lead to a completely new conception of the nature of the universe for philosophy and for the other sciences as well. Bertrand Russell ended the domination of ordinary grammar over logical analyses, which means in effect that what is existing must be independent of and different from the way in which it is arbitrarily presented to us in words and the sentences they form. He insists that in future the laws of grammar shall not be allowed to dominate ontology. It is really no matter for surprise to learn that during his investigations into the various ways in which language leads us into error he toyed with the idea of developing a perfect language which would be an accurate reflection of reality.

These years in which he devoted himself to abstract thought were a period of spiritual asceticism for him. His analysis of logic produced more and more subtle distinctions. But the more and more complicated logic itself became, the more difficult it also became to use it for the purpose of providing proof. Doubts as to the scope of logic now aroused doubt as to the precepts of the ancient philosophers, who had relied on it unquestioningly. Bertrand Russell pointed out that all logical assumptions could always only be hypothetical since each one always went back to an 'if'. Ultimate assertions concerning the existing world were therefore impossible. Logic was not in a position to enable science to provide proof for any kind of existence. The only way in which to arrive at an abstract knowledge of at least the physical world was to develop an effective logical technique by including mathematics. In accordance with the nature of mathematical logic Bertrand Russell now decided in favour of the empirical method based on analysis. With this method only one problem can be examined at a time, but this did not greatly disturb him since he has always preferred the small truth to the large nebulosity.

Ultimate questions of value can naturally not be settled in such a strictly scientific fashion, and Bertrand Russell has therefore banished them to the sphere of feeling and emotion. Under the influence of Santayana he now abandoned his original conviction – which he still upheld in his book *Problems of Philosophy*, published in 1912, that in ethical matters we are able to rely on *a priori* knowledge. According to Santayana good and evil are always a matter of personal belief, and to illustrate his point he quotes the example of whisky, which does more harm than coffee, but is not on that account already 'drunk in the bottle'. One should therefore never ascribe an impersonal attribute to a thing, but should always characterize the attribute as one's own personal thought.

As knowledge can be gained only through science we must restrict ourselves to such truth as can be attained by scientific methods. Science is not in a position to set up generally valid moral standards. It cannot, for example, prove that the cruelty practised by dictators is unjust; nor, however, can it prove the contrary. Every for and against is always a personal decision. From now on Bertrand Russell made no secret of his personal feelings, though from his standpoint as a scientist he had to admit that it was impossible to cut the ground from under anyone's feet merely by scientific reasoning.

He was a thorough-going rationalist, and in his mistrust of any and every irrational feeling, and of all mystical and idealistic tendencies, he himself became almost a mystic of rationalism. He was above all anxious to free philosophy from 'the desire for edification', since its association with theories concerning the nature of the universe had distorted the features of philosophy for hundreds of years. In his book *A History of Western Philosophy*, first published in 1945, he writes:

'Intellectually, the effect of mistaken moral considerations upon philosophy has been to impede progress to an extraordinary extent. I do not myself believe that philosophy can either prove or disprove the truth of religious dogmas, but ever since Plato most philosophers have considered it part of their business to produce 'proofs' of immortality and the existence of God. They have found fault with the proofs of their predecessors – Saint Thomas rejected Saint Anselm's proof, and Kant rejected Descartes' – but they have supplied new ones of their own. In order to make their proofs seem valid, they have had to falsify logic, to make mathematics mystical, and to pretend that deep-seated prejudices were heaven-sent intuitions.'[1]

Bertrand Russell condemns such behaviour as 'a kind of treachery', and in his view a philosopher must use his professional competence for nothing but 'a disinterested search for truth'. 'The true philosopher' must be prepared 'to examine *all* preconceptions'. In Bertrand Russell's view only investigation which is free of all personal influences, which is strictly truthful, and which renounces fanaticism in any form can provide the necessary conditions in which philosophy can blossom in the interests of all mankind. In particular he insists that a scientific philosophy must be ethically neutral. If it is, he admits, it will certainly offer 'less glitter of outward mirage to flatter fallacious hopes', but at the same time it will be 'more indifferent to fate,

[1] *A History of Western Philosophy*, Allen & Unwin, London, p. 835.

and more capable of accepting the world without the tyrannous imposition of our human and temporary demands.'[2]

Apart from his philosophical outlook Bertrand Russell was also impelled by biological considerations to ask: 'Is there anything in the process of evolution that demands the hypothesis of a purpose, whether immanent or transcendent? This is the crucial question. For one who is not a biologist it is difficult to speak otherwise than with hesitation on this question; I am, however, entirely unconvinced by the arguments in favour of purpose I have seen.'[3]

[2] *Mysticism and Logic*, George Allen & Unwin, 1917, p. 46.
[3] *The Scientific Outlook*, George Allen & Unwin, 1931, p. 127.

4 Politics and People

DESPITE the tremendous amount of sheer hard work involved in the writing of *Principia Mathematica*, Bertrand Russell was also active in this period as a writer and critic in scientific journals, and particularly as a reviewer for the philosophic journal *Mind*. Almost all the abstruse philosophical works published in German, French and Italian in this period found their way onto his writing desk for review. He would invariably report soberly and objectively on what he had read, but now and again, whilst always remaining just, he could be merciless.

One might suppose that a man engaged in writing a book like *Principia Mathematica* would withdraw as far as possible into private life for the purpose, and that in such circumstances the reading of other scientific books would be regarded as nothing but a supplement to his own scientific work, but this was certainly not the case with Bertrand Russell, who, in addition to his writing and reading, took an active part in politics as well. In fact, it was in sociology and politics that his own lively temperament found that necessary day to day relief that he strictly refused to allow himself in his philosophic thought. Those practical and moral considerations which he allowed no place in the realm of philosophy were transferred to daily life. He was, for example, a member of a group known as the 'Co-efficients', and he spoke publicly on Liberal platforms in favour of Free Trade. He also decided to make a bid to enter parliament so in 1907 he presented himself to the electorate in Wimbledon as a Liberal enjoying the support of the National Union of Women's Suffrage Societies, and during his campaign he spoke vigorously in favour of votes for women, supporting the more moderate group of the movement which sought to obtain the franchise for women by legal and constitutional means. He felt that the Liberal ideals of democracy, liberty and justice clearly included equal rights for women in political and social life. It did not greatly disturb either himself or his wife to find themselves the target for mockery on the part of those who opposed women's suffrage, though they were even physically assaulted on occasions, and once an egg hurled by an opponent broke in her face.

In those days elections were fought out on the streets, and wireless and television were still far away in the future. As no one thought even remotely of war, foreign-political questions were not in the forefront of the battle, and the issues at stake were all domestic. One of the most important of them for Bertrand Russell was this question of votes for women. Despite his eloquence on the hustings, when the votes came to be counted, Bertrand Russell was seen to have been defeated by his Conservative opponent.

In 1910 when *Principia Mathematica* was practically finished he once again put himself forward as a candidate for parliament, and this time he might well have been elected, but his enemies made great play with his irreligious attitude, and this turned even his own supporters away from him.

Although Bertrand Russell was always quite willing to admit that his political opinions found no justification in his philosophy, his entry into practical politics in favour of the liberty of the individual and the general welfare of the community was nevertheless quite in accordance with his view that philosophic questions which logic was powerless to answer could be settled only by personal temperament.

Hegel's view that the interests of the state must always have priority over those of the individual had few if any supporters in British politics, but in Germany and Italy it was to provide the extremist right wings with a theoretical basis for their policies after the 1914-1918 War.

Because, by analogy with his philosophic tendency he stressed the individual and the empirical, Bertrand Russell could change his opinion in political matters with astonishing rapidity. His considered judgements ignored any personal feelings he might have concerning a question and they were based strictly on the given facts. The constantly changing state of world affairs thus meant that he was always expressing opinions in accordance with the given situation at any particular time. And he certainly had no use for any political theory which claimed to have a monopoly of wisdom, and it is from this standpoint that his own political writings must be judged. He had certain advantages over most professional politicians. He never got blindly caught up in anything, but first examined the case for each side from a distance and as a disinterested party. Only then did he decide in favour of the one or the other. It would be no easy matter to reconcile Bertrand Russell's political attitudes even approximately. All you would find would be similarities in the reasoning leading him from one camp into the other. But one thing has never changed: his advocacy of Liberal principles. For example, at the outbreak of the Boer war he first supported his own country, but when he observed the struggle for power which was going on behind the scenes, and realized the cruelty to the innocent that was resulting from it, he quickly changed his mind.

He understood the tragic loneliness and isolation in which most people spend their lives, and he desired to do everything he possibly could to ameliorate it. His essay 'Free Man's Worship' deals with this problem at some length:

'The life of man is a long march through the night, surrounded by invisible foes, tortured by weariness and pain, towards a goal that few can hope to reach, and where none may tarry long. One by one, as they march, our comrades vanish from our sight, seized by the silent orders of omnipotent death. Very brief is the time in which we can help them, in which their happiness or misery is decided. Be it ours to shed sunshine on their path, to lighten their sorrows by the balm of sympathy, to give them the pure joy of a never-tiring affection, to strengthen their failing courage, to instil faith in their hours of despair.'[1]

[1] Quoted from *Philosophical Essays*, Longmans, Green & Co., 1910, p. 69. *A Free Man's Worship* is published by George Allen & Unwin Ltd.

In his book *Marriage and Morals*, published in 1929, Bertrand Russell expressed his views on this particular aspect of the relations of the sexes. Early in the present century, when his own marriage was no longer so satisfactory, he began to have his own private ideas on the subject. The religious zeal of the Quakers was strong in his wife Alys, and it tended to make her turn her sympathy for the weak and the oppressed into a heaven-sent mission. Russell's lively and objective mind, his dislike of solemnity, and of being bored or of boring other people, and his trenchant irony made him a bad subject for this sort of thing. Although, in one way and another, a good deal was at stake for him if he were divorced, he preferred that his wife should put an end to their marriage rather than that they should live on together now that marriage no longer represented the state of their feelings for each other. Such an attitude was incomprehensible to people of his own class, and he had to make up his mind that if his marriage broke up he would encounter social difficulties. The hostility which now began to gather against him was increased by his demonstrative pacifism when the clouds of war began to mass on the horizon. The result was social ostracism in his own class, so he now began to seek the friendship of people who were more broad-minded in their views. As he was already a well-known figure he had to put up with the criticism and condemnation of society, which, incidentally, did not look with a very friendly eye on his brother either, because Frank was living up to the promise of his early years and his life was very turbulent. He was married three times and found himself in prison on one occasion for alleged bigamy. In fact he became known as 'The Wicked Duke', and he was mixed up in all sorts of business affairs that brought him to the verge of ruin. In short, neither of the two Russell brothers was now regarded as altogether *comme il faut*. It was a very long time before Bertrand could finally free himself from his marriage. From 1911 onwards the couple lived apart, but it was not until 1921 that they were actually divorced. In retrospect it is only just to Alys to say that while they did live together as man and wife she gave him the atmosphere in which he could follow the fundamental ideas of his life in tranquillity.

When the day's work was over Bertrand liked to dance, and occasionally he also played tennis, but his special pleasure was walking. Whilst doing fifteen or twenty miles a day in the company of friends he could talk the whole time about mathematics and philosophy. Even when he visited other countries he still went on long walking tours. In his circle of friends everyone was comfortably off and with sufficient money to spend his free time just as he pleased. Such people had plenty of spare time for their personal interests, and after working in the morning they would visit each other in their country houses in the afternoon, go on walking tours together, and talk endlessly about the things in which they were most interested. The Russells visited the Shaws and the Webbs, and each shared to some extent in the work and pleasures of the other. They amused themselves with the carefully calculated vegetarian dietetic systems worked out by Beatrice Webb; Bernard Shaw would practise standing on his head, and Bertrand Russell would do cartwheels. Sidney Webb, who was a rather solemn man, would often shake his head over Bertrand's little jokes, taking them in all seriousness. The circle in which Bertrand Russell now moved suited him admirably since it consisted of people of advanced views who mistrusted all traditions.

One of Bertrand Russell's close friends was Gilbert Murray, who had married one of Bertrand's cousins. Gilbert Murray had translated the *Hippolytus* of Euripides, a performance that Bertrand Russell greatly admired. In order to be near the Murrays the Russells now moved to Bagley Wood near Oxford. Bertrand Russell was also attracted to Oxford because it was the stronghold of his philosophical opponents, the idealists, and he was anxious to make their acquaintance and meet them in discussion. But it wasn't long before he began to dislike Oxford intensely, partly for its philosophical idealism and partly because of its neglect of the natural sciences. He was fond of saying that the only man in the place who knew anything at all about mathematical logic was C. G. Berry, an unconsidered librarian, who is mentioned in *Principia Mathematica*. Once he had formed an unfavourable opinion Bertrand Russell saw no reason to conceal it, and on one occasion he observed that the new gasometer, whose erection was fluttering the Oxford dovecotes at the time, was clearly the only source of light there.

He was also generous with high-spirited and witty contributions to the discussions of the Aristotelian Society, whose president he was for a while. This was the time when he shaved off his moustache for good, thereby greatly altering his appearance. And, if you can believe him, this freeing of his upper lip from its hirsute covering also changed his character. At least it was certainly now easier to observe the rather cynical curl of his lip than it had been before.

Ottoline Morrell, half-sister to the Duke of Portland, lived in Garsington House near Oxford, and she and Bertrand Russell became very close friends. Unconventional herself, she nevertheless played a role in society, and she was always on the look out for new artistic and other talent. She proceeded on her way accompanied by a cloud of anecdotes, some of them true, others not, and her striking appearance – she was a tall, slim woman with auburn hair who always dressed eccentrically – lent colour to them both. Her knowledge of literature and her judgement of art were both very sound, and invitations to her house were highly valued, since one was always sure of meeting a circle of interesting and entertaining people.

5 At Cambridge and Harvard

FROM the year 1910 on Bertrand Russell lectured at Cambridge on logic and the principles of mathematics. His lectures were not particularly well attended, and most of his listeners were people who, like himself, were engaged in scientific work – though at least this meant that he could be quite sure that the ideas he expressed in his lectures were not falling on stony ground. This was the time when Alfred Whitehead left Cambridge, and G. E. Moore and Wittgenstein arrived. John Maynard Keynes, who subsequently became best known as an economist, was also a member of the philosophical circle which was to set the standards in Cambridge for many years to come.

Wittgenstein came of a well-to-do Austrian family. At first on arriving in England he had gone to Manchester because he was then primarily interested in machinery and particularly in aircraft engineering. The necessity of occupying himself with mathematical formulae in connection with the designing of aero-engines and propellers developed in him a love of mathematics.

Russell's reputation as a leading exponent of the principles of mathematics soon drew Wittgenstein to Cambridge. A dissertation he wrote on a philosophical

D

theme at Russell's suggestion revealed that he had abilities as a philosopher. The two were soon spending whole nights together discussing mathematical logic. Wittgenstein was a rather solemn type who tended to take everything literally, and he was very astonished at the relationship between G. E. Moore and Bertrand Russell, since, as he was aware, the two didn't care much for each other, and yet they constantly sought each other's company for discussions. Russell records that when a discussion began Wittgenstein always threatened that he would commit suicide when it ended. Altogether he must have made a strange impression on the more phlegmatic British. Amongst the well-known figures at Cambridge G. E. Moore was the only opponent worthy of Russell's steel in a discussion. Those who listened to them went away with the impression that Moore was interested only in getting at the truth, whereas Bertrand Russell often struck them as trying to coruscate with witty antitheses. Moore certainly enjoyed a great reputation at Cambridge. Bertrand Russell also greatly admired the razor-sharp mind of Keynes, though he disapproved of his contempt for the common man. At that time at least Bertrand Russell believed that common sense really was common.

As a public speaker his wit and irony always fascinated his audiences. His criticism of Bergson's mystical evolutionary philosophy won him general approval, not only amongst the public, but also amongst his colleagues. This criticism can be read today in his book *A History of Western Philosophy*. His own philosophic position at the time can be seen from his book *Prob-*

lems of Philosophy which he wrote for the Home University Library, but subsequently he was to change his opinions in many respects, and for this reason it is very difficult to classify him with any particular philosophic school. Each time he changed his views he was always ready with very subtle reasons to explain his attitude, and as he grew older this became more and more obvious. What the inquiring observer finds is a labyrinth of differing opinions all calculated to shock him. We are accustomed to associating a particular theory or doctrine with the name of a philosopher, and it was usually the ambition of philosophers to defend their own particular systems against all others by every means in their power, but Bertrand Russell has never adopted such an attitude and has always regarded it as vanity. He would often dismiss his own, perhaps quite recently formed, views as summarily as though they were those of someone else. In such cases his motive was always a fanatical devotion to truth, and he was quite prepared to accept the fact that his own words could often be quoted against him. He could, it is true, afford to do this sort of thing because his writings on logic had already assured him a place amongst the great thinkers. By a process of successive approximation philosophy and the natural sciences reach a point where they meet and touch. Proof of this is provided by Einstein's theory of relativity.

In 1914 Bertrand Russell was preparing to give a series of lectures in Boston on the subject of 'Our Knowledge of the External World'. Before leaving for the United States he tried out one or two of these lectures in Cambridge, and he was a trifle disconcerted to find that about ten times as many people seemed interested in his theory of perception as were interested in his mathematical lectures. Because he won his audiences by his wit and brilliance many people supposed that he was a born orator, but this was not so, and in those days at least, he still suffered from stage fright.

As we have seen, he did not keep to one system, but he did keep to one method, that of 'Occam's razor', which is summed up in the axiom 'the number of entities should not be unnecessarily increased'. His analytical method was to cut out everything he regarded as unimportant and to hold fast to the rest as being all that was necessary for understanding. He regarded this method of elimination as a guarantee that his results would approximate as near as possible to experience. Our senses provide a direct acquaintance with the entities in the form of 'sense-data'. Thoughts, feelings, the ego and general ideas are also directly accessible. But what is perceived is only indirectly accessible by way of description. The things of daily life, physical objects and other minds, are known only by description. By analysis he comes to the conclusion that the appearances of things, sensations and images, are real, but that the thing itself is a logical construction, like 'substance' or 'matter'. In scientific philosophy logical constructions take the place of inferred entities. Sense-data form the basis for these logical constructions. Later on 'events', the content of perception, were added to sensations as a basis for what was concluded from them. At this point Bertrand Russell was reproached for having insufficiently defined the frontier between the physical and the psychical. But his belief in his method remained unshaken, and he was convinced that this alone guaranteed the accuracy of his philosophic analysis. He paid his first visit to the United States shortly before the outbreak of the first world war, and he was delighted at the readiness he found there to follow up his new philosophical ideas. Apart from his official lectures he also held a private course on symbolic logic for interested students. On the whole he did not find that he could rate the intelligence of his students very highly. The only two who were, in his recollection, above average were a certain T. S. Eliot and a Greek named Raphael Demos. Later on Demos was to hold the chair of philosophy at Harvard – and what T. S. Eliot became everyone knows. Both were regular guests at the tea parties Bertrand Russell used to give because their informal atmosphere allowed him to chat to his students about the subject of his course. T. S. Eliot found it amusing to juggle with mathematical symbols, though feeling that this diversion had very little to do with reality. Shortly after Bertrand Russell returned to England he met Eliot again, and as at this period of his life Eliot was hard up, Bertrand Russell gave him quarters in his own house. When Eliot got married Bertrand Russell extended his hospitality to the wife as well. He also provided Eliot with letters of recommendation so that before long he was writing reviews for the leading philosophical journals. When Bertrand Russell moved to a house at Marlow the Eliots went along too, and the discussions they had were certainly not without their effect on Eliot's poetry. Eliot adopted Bertrand Russell's ideas as warmly as Bertrand had adopted him and his wife, and his review of *Mysticism and Logic* was the only one to meet with favour in Bertrand Russell's eyes.

6 The First World War and Prison

THE outbreak of the first world war made a shattering impression on Bertrand Russell. Abruptly he was forced to realize that his belief in the essential reasonableness and common sense of man was an error, and he was now compelled to witness the enthusiasm with which apparently sane men were concocting plans for the speediest possible destruction of their fellow men. And this was going on amongst the civilized peoples of the West! He quickly recovered from his preliminary dismay, and soon he was speaking out openly against the war, a very daring thing to do in those emotional days. He argued that the crime of sacrificing the lives of human beings, the crime of maiming young men, was far worse than a pacifist submission to Hohenzollern Germany would be. His work for the cause of peace now took up most of his time and he realized that his scientific interests represented only one facet of his life. His opposition to the war caused him to be denounced as unpatriotic and as a bad Englishman. This, of course, was very unjust. He loved his country dearly, and he even desired her victory, but truth meant even more to him, and, in particular, he was filled with a profound mistrust of those traditional ideas which cloaked the savagery of war with the false glamour of honour and heroism. He felt that killing had nothing to do with heroism, and that courage whipped up by patriotic propaganda had nothing to do with honour. He felt that the war would end in mutual crippling, but not in mutual destruction. Both Britain and Germany would survive the war, and ultimately they would both recover – which meant that the whole senseless game could start up all over again.

In his *Portraits from Memory*, published in 1956, he justifies the opinions he held during the first world war, to which he was particularly opposed because he felt certain that it would inevitably drag a second in its train; and he felt that all the excesses of Bolshevism, Fascism and Hitlerism developed from it with the inevitability of a Greek tragedy. He realized that Britain's neutrality would have made a German victory inevitable, but the war would have been short, and the United States could have kept out of it. Recalling his own experiences, Bertrand Russell insisted that Hohenzollern Germany was a great deal freer before the war than most countries were after the war, with the exception of Britain and Scandinavia, and he felt sure that in the event of victory Germany's progressive forces would never have allowed National Socialism to triumph. Instead, freedom had greatly diminished as the result of the first world war whilst militarism had grown much stronger.

Amongst British pacifists there were, of course, people who gladly seized on anti-war propaganda as an outlet for their general dissatisfaction; and these included extremists like D. H. Lawrence, who got into touch with Bertrand Russell. Lawrence wanted a complete social revolution, with the nationalization of industry and everything that went with it. Bertrand Russell made public speeches against the war, wrote regularly in *The Labour Leader*, and became a member of the No-Conscription Fellowship, which developed into the organizational centre of those who were opposed to the war.

A favourite meeting place for the intellectual pacifists of Britain was Ottoline Morrell's house in London or in the country. They never got any further than long and involved discussions, and some of them were uncomfortable in Bertrand Russell's presence. They found his mixture of rationalism and cynicism irritating, and they often felt that his barbs of wit and wisdom had a disagreeable personal point. Bertrand Russell himself enjoyed the gatherings at Ottoline Morrell's house and he was grateful for her hospitality. He also appreciated her goodness. Both were treated with mockery by some of her literary guests. Even Asquith, the Prime Minister of the day, was sometimes to be seen at her house, though it swarmed with pacifists. Aldous Huxley was another regular visitor.

In the meantime both his colleagues and the undergraduates at Cambridge made Bertrand Russell feel their disapproval. His attitude was too radical and uncompromising for them, even though they did not always reject his ideas. It must also be remembered that there was very little of the traditional apostle of peace about him, and many people found him unbearably aggressive, though he was anxious to enlist as much support as possible in the war of words and ideas he was now fighting. The Everett case demonstrated that he was quite prepared to stand by his convictions and take the responsibility for his actions. Everett was a young pacifist who, having been called up for military service, refused to obey orders. For this he was tried and sentenced to two years hard labour. The No-Conscription Fellowship issued a leaflet on his behalf, and a number of its members were arrested for distributing it, brought before the courts and themselves sentenced to terms of imprisonment. Bertrand Russell now wrote a letter to *The Times* protesting and at the same time revealing that he was the author of the leaflet in question. He was now charged himself and brought to trial. At the request of the censorship authorities the proceedings were not generally reported, since it was feared that Bertrand Russell's spirited defence might cause alarm and despondency amongst the general public. He was convicted and fined a hundred pounds.

This conviction and his general unpopularity did not cause him to waver, but the sequel did hit him very hard. His old College, Trinity, of which he was now a Fellow, decided that it wanted no more to do with its errant son, and he was dismissed. This expulsion from the circle of Cambridge scholars and scientists was difficult to bear, but he was certainly guilty of exaggeration when he subsequently spoke of the wave of hatred that beat against him, though he was made to feel general disapproval and hostility.

After this deeply wounding experience the radicalism of his views on war was transferred to all other spheres of human existence, beginning with marriage, taking in the Government and religion on the way, and

going on to educational matters. What he had to say on
these subjects was incorporated in a book published
in 1916 entitled *Principles of Social Reconstruction*.
It was based largely on lectures he had given in Cambridge before being cast out.

This was the year in which he made the acquaintance
of Stanley Unwin, who was already well on the way to
becoming a leading figure in the publishing world,
and who was later to be rewarded with a knighthood
for his services to literature. Unwin was one of the
directors of George Allen & Unwin, a firm he had
founded at the very outbreak of the war. Having been
impressed by a number of Bertrand Russell's articles
he now proposed that they should be published in
book form, and he hoped to be able to persuade his
fellow directors to agree with him. The time was just
about as unpromising as it possibly could have been,
and at first they refused. Then Professor Muirhead,
the editor of the *Library of Philosophy*, pronounced
in favour of the book, declaring that it was a philosophical contribution of very considerable importance,
so finally they agreed. The book, *Principles of Social
Reconstruction*, has not lost its importance down to
the present day. It was also remarkable as being the
first of Bertrand Russell's books to enjoy a wider sale.
With it he emerged from the exclusive circle of academic life and presented himself to a more general
public – not only in his own country, but throughout
the world. He felt that it was his mission in life to help
humanity with his ideas, to open men's eyes to the
hindrances that barred the way to their happiness, and
to show them what steps they must take in order to

attain it. The tremendous cataclysm of war was undoubtedly directly responsible for urging him into
this role.

So far as the spread of his more popularly understood
ideas was concerned he had a good deal for which to
thank Stanley Unwin. Unwin used his abilities and his
connections in the international publishing world to
launch Bertrand Russell on a successful literary career.
A good deal of Unwin's experience had been gained
from a long stay in Germany, and the detailed knowledge of the publishing business he obtained in this
way was coupled with a flair for sensing and opening
up new book markets. He established valuable connections both with publishers and booksellers in journeys
all over the world, and now he used his influence and
organization to spread Bertrand Russell's fame throughout the world. Encouraged by the fascination of his
more popularly-written works many readers now ven-
tured into the deeper waters of abstruse philosophical
problems. In Germany he was certainly more widely
read than any other English philosopher.

His expulsion from academic circles at Cambridge
also involved a financial loss, and he now had to cast
around to find an income elsewhere. Friends recall
that he was so painfully short of money at this time
that he often had to borrow the few coppers he needed
for the bus fare to enable him to attend the meetings
of the No-Conscription Fellowship. Even merely attend-
ing such meetings was quite a risky business. The
police kept a close watch and from time to time they
would arrest the more radical speakers. Russell felt
himself as the friend and protector of these coura-

geous young men, and he did all he could to help them.

He now decided to hold a series of lectures throughout the country in the hope of supplementing his financial resources. The first lecture was to deal with the philosophical basis of politics. He was naturally too well known to be able to do anything unobtrusively, and the War Office immediately forbade him to enter the militarily proscribed area along the coast, in which many important towns were situated. Pacifists were regarded with such irrational mistrust that it was even thought that if they were allowed near the coast they might signal to lurking German submarines. In Bertrand Russell's case the authorities felt that his public appearances might lead to disturbances amongst munition workers, and perhaps to strikes. It was time, they thought, for such a dangerous person to be restrained.

Bertrand Russell himself gave the authorities the opportunity they needed in the shape of a very outspoken article in *Tribunal,* the organ of the No-Conscription Fellowship. Oddly enough it happened just when he had decided to withdraw from active work in the pacifist movement, because the war was now obviously coming to an end and he felt that it would be better if he retired into the background to draft proposals for measures to be put into operation in the subsequent period of reconstruction. However, at the request of the editor of *Tribunal* he wrote the fatal article prophesying famine throughout Europe as the result of the war, and a battle of all against all. Even in the event of an Allied victory U.S. troops would continue to occupy Britain and France in order to suppress strikes. And for good measure he added that they already had some experience of strike-breaking in their own country. Not, he admitted, that it was likely that such ideas found any place in the minds of the British Government, which seemed to be bereft of any ideas at all!

The authorities were, of course, used to being insulted by Bertrand Russell, but this was going too far and specifically insulted Britain's chief ally, so at the beginning of 1918 Bertrand Russell found himself once again in the dock. The incriminating article was read in court as evidence, to be welcomed with loud applause from the public benches – which did not prevent a conviction and a sentence of six months imprisonment. Leave to appeal was refused, and in May 1918 Bertrand Russell began to serve his sentence in Brixton Prison.

His stay in prison turned out to be very useful and not particularly disagreeable. At first the prison authorities proposed to treat him very strictly, but influential friends got busy behind the scenes, and so he came into the Second Division, where he was allowed to read and write. His brother Frank was particularly active on his behalf and used all his connections to ameliorate Bertrand's lot, so that before long his cell was provided with some comforts, including a carpet on the floor and a writing desk. The unusual prisoner lived according to a strict work schedule devised by himself: four hours writing daily on philosophical matters, four hours philosophical reading, and four hours recreational reading. Once a week he was allowed a visit from three people, and these friends were received in the prison yard. These meetings gave him a great deal of pleasure, particularly as they represented the only way in which he could get news of what was going on in the outside world.

The one thing he missed, and longed for, was intelligent conversation, and in his enforced isolation this seemed to him to be the very stuff of human liberty. Although in his usual quiet and ironical way he seemed to find imprisonment no very great burden he nevertheless longed to get away from the imprisoning walls into the countryside with his friends. He compared himself to a valuable book someone had bought and put away on the shelf unread. One thing this term of imprisonment certainly did was to reinforce his passionate love of liberty. If men's minds remained free then all repressive violence must fail. Subsequently he declared that during his imprisonment he had revelled in his memories of the wonderful places he had been to and of the fascinating experiences he had had. He longed for the whole world to be as free as his mind.

Whilst he was in prison he wrote his *Introduction to Mathematical Philosophy*, which was published in 1919. He was released from prison shortly before the end of the war, and as in the meantime the call-up age had been extended in order to provide more manpower, he was now faced with the likelihood of being called up for military service. Teaching was, however, a scheduled occupation, so that if he became a teacher he would be exempt. The idea was that he should give a series of lectures and thus qualify, but he hadn't enough money to finance the tour, pay his travelling

expenses and provide his keep. The money he had inherited would have sufficed to keep him modestly, but
he had always expended it liberally to help friends and
contribute to scientific projects and good works. Now
was the time for his friends to rally round him, and
this they did to such purpose that he was able to
undertake three years' teaching activity. He started
at once with lectures on the analysis of mind, a subject
for which he had prepared himself during his stay in
Brixton Prison. He did not want to be dependent on
his friends when the war ended and he intended to
rely on his ability to earn a living with his pen.

His preliminary analysis of mind led to a philosophical rapprochement between mind and matter, and he
came to the conclusion that they both derived from
some common substance, the ultimate constituents of
both being of the same nature. This view brought him
close to the position of the American philosopher William James, and where perception is concerned his
new attitude can be summed up in the term 'neutral
monism'. His book *The Analysis of Mind*, containing
these theories, was published in 1921, and to some
extent it runs parallel to his other book *Our Knowledge of the External World* in which he had previously come to the conclusion that matter is a logical
construction based on sense-data, and he now applied
the same conclusion to mind, and defined it too as a
logical construction based on sense-data. The final
conclusion reads: sense-data and sensations are identical.

This contradicted the views he had previously expressed when he was striving to establish a clear dis-

tinction between mind and matter and had scoffed at Bergson for confusing the two.

However, Bertrand Russell's attitude to this problem cannot be described as Behaviourism, since Behaviourism denies the existence of mind altogether and contends that man and his functions consist entirely of matter. Einstein revised the earlier crude conception of matter and mass since it no longer stood up to the new ideas in physics and psychology. Mind now lost some of its aura of independence, and matter was no longer thought of as something subordinate and inferior. Bertrand Russell carefully studied the new physics, and began at once to consider the philosophical consequences. Einstein seemed to come nearest to neutral monism, but nevertheless Bertrand Russell did not succeed in finding confirmation in Einstein's theories of his belief that mind and matter are one, and the best he could do was to establish that both mind and matter are based on 'sensations' or 'sense-data'; which act as the link between them. As certain individual functions of mind escaped this simple construction there was still to some extent dualism.

Russell frankly admitted that he was not in a position to prove the dependence of mind on physical laws.

E

7 Journeys to Soviet Russia and China

THE news of the Russian Revolution was received with great enthusiasm by British Socialists, and their sympathies were so strong for the new régime that they tended to idealize its leaders and overlook their claim to totalitarian power. In the meantime Bertrand Russell had joined the Socialist camp, but his critical faculties remained as keen as ever, and he was not prepared to accept this adulation. For him Socialism must abolish Capitalism by transferring the means of production to those who are engaged in it, and he looked with misgiving at any form of Socialism that tended to increase the power of the State.

At first, however, he openly sided with the Russian Revolution and was delighted at its success, particularly as it was favourably influencing the situation in Germany and Austria, and even stirring up men's minds in Britain. The United States was the one country he regarded as hopeless in this respect.

He was naturally anxious to see what the situation was for himself on the spot and so when a Labour Party delegation set off for Soviet Russia in May 1920 he attached himself to it as an unofficial observer. The members of the delegation were greeted at the frontier as princes had once been greeted, and the reception was repeated wherever they went in their special train with its red bunting and revolutionary slogans. They were the guests of honour at splendid banquets, there were quartered in historic palaces, and the only evidence of the proletarian revolution was the constant playing of the 'Internationale' by military bands.

The delegates were introduced to Trotsky, and Bertrand Russell was forcibly reminded of Napoleon. Trotsky's soldierly appearance, his keen eyes, his fine head and his great intelligence fascinated all who came into contact with him. But Bertrand Russell kept his head as he was accustomed to do. The stories about Trotsky did not impress him one way or the other. and he judged that the man was more vain than power seeking, and he felt that he was more likely to be cruel through lack of consideration than to be so deliberately. Lenin, on the other hand, struck him as a much quieter and more solid type. There was nothing in his appearance or his behaviour to indicate the great power he undoubtedly wielded.

The thing that deeply shocked Bertrand Russell was the dire poverty and misery of ordinary people. There were endless queues for a little black bread, and to obtain even the simplest article of clothing, indeed, any consumer goods at all, was hopeless. Life was depressed down to the level of sheer existence, and as far as Bertrand Russell was concerned this did a great deal to tarnish the bright colours in which the ideals of the revolution were being presented. People in Britain had a very different picture of what Socialism ought to look like. As it was, Bertrand Russell had the impression that all joy, all beauty and all human liberty had been banished from this world. However, as poor as it was, life did go forward in a framework of law and order and he saw no evidence of any excesses. On his return it was quite clear that he had definitely been cured of any tendency to uncritical enthusiasm. What he had to say to his fellow country-men about his visit was put into his book *The Practice and Theory of Bolshevism*, published in 1920. It sums up the *pros* and the *cons* of Bolshevism very fairly, but the balance undoubtedly tips in its dis-favour.

He was in no doubt, of course, about the significance of the event, and he was aware that the new system of society which had been born in Russia would mean a very great deal to the rest of the world, but he doubted very much whether a revolution born of hunger and misery would ever contribute much to human wisdom. Such a basis was unsuitable for the realization of those high ideals every new order of society needed.

Most British Socialists thought that the revolution-ary government in Russia was just another otherwise normal government but one based on Socialist prin-ciples, but Bertrand Russell pointed out that the dictatorship of the proletariat was not a mere form of words, and that what existed in Russia was really a dictatorship, and one prepared to adopt any means to maintain itself. He denounced intolerance and fanati-cism because they made men blind to the misery and wretchedness of their fellow men. Bolshevism had become an end in itself, and it was now altogether in-different to the effects of its rule on the welfare of the individual. Such fanaticism could only result in the increase of human suffering and not its amelioration. Bolshevism had taken on the character of a religion and it was falling into all the old mistakes that Christianity had once made. Bertrand Russell was one of the first to compare Bolshevism with a religion. Bolshevism was not identical with the Communist Party, a branch of which had just been formed in Great Britain and was regarded by British Socialists as just one party amongst others. Bertrand Russell's final conclusion was that he would be sorry to see any form of Communist government in Britain since it was, he felt, in complete contradiction to the British character.

There were not many Socialists in Britain prepared to recognize the justification for such severe strictures, and once again Bertrand Russell's uncompromising frankness made him the target for angry attacks, just as it had done during the war from the other side.

Incidentally, the problems of Bertrand Russell's own personality clearly expressed themselves in his criticism of Bolshevism. Two very different facets of character are in constant conflict in his personality. There is, on one hand, the cool, objective scientist interested in nothing but the truth and prepared to let it lead him where it might, and, on the other, there is the philanthropist who is deeply conscious of his share of the responsibility for the welfare of society. His experiences in Soviet Russia had filled him with a horror of the masses, and in his own words he feared nothing so much as the blind herd. He was firmly convinced that only the individual would ever produce anything worth while, but he also felt strongly that the individual must feel responsibility for the welfare of the whole, and that, in fact, this welfare would depend in the last resort on the integrity of the individual. Because of this viewpoint he always felt a deep need to have friends around him with whom he could talk and to whom he could listen, and with whom he could discuss what measures he regarded as necessary for the betterment of the world. But how was he as a private individual to exercise any effective influence beyond his own small circle? Clearly, anyone who was interested in the fate of the world must take part in some way or other in politics. On the other hand, membership of a political party invariably led sooner or later to dogmatism, and was thus at odds with the objective search for truth. For this reason Bertrand Russell felt that the intellectual should keep himself independent of parties, whilst nevertheless always being prepared to intervene in political matters whenever the cause of truth seemed to make such intervention desirable. Political decisions were taken in the name of all, and the responsibility involved went far beyond the competence of the professional politician. This independent attitude served Bertrand Russell very well on the whole. When he criticized from a distance and independent of any party or group he usually hit the nail on the head, but as soon as he made himself the mouthpiece of any particular group he would find himself hampered, if ever so little, by *parti pris*.

Although holding such views he was by no means free of the longing to associate himself with like-minded people in their enthusiasms, and when he felt himself isolated his reaction was usually over-sensitive. For example, the unfavourable reaction of his Socialist friends to his objective analysis of the situation in Soviet Russia depressed him at the time, but later on he was to have the satisfaction of seeing his book republished almost without alteration. This was during the Second World War (1939-45), and in the long meantime all his prophecies had come true and all his judgements had proved accurate.

Shortly after this direct encounter with Bolshevism he began to make preparations for another long journey. The governors of Pekin University had invited him to give a course of lectures to its students, and he gladly accepted. He was accompanied on this trip by Miss Dora Black, a young lady whom he had known and with whom he had worked for some time. She was a lively, forceful character, and very much younger than Bertrand Russell. On their return from China she was to become the second Mrs Russell.

Bertrand Russell was delighted with China, but he was well aware that it was a dying China, and he deeply deplored her decline. He greatly valued the freedom of the individual in this Eastern country, and he felt that only a long civilized people were capable of arriving at it. Government took a back seat and left the individual free to develop. The Chinese were not subject to the commandments of any dogmatic religion, and they were free to practise the virtues of dignity, self-control and *politesse* inherited from their forbears. Bertrand Russell enjoyed and approved what he saw and experienced in China, and as a private individual he was free to enjoy the aesthetic side of both the noble past and the very agreeable present. As a far-sighted thinker he did not, of course, fail to see the dangers that were closing in on this China and threatening its existence, and he drafted a number of constructive proposals by which he hoped the country would succeed in extricating itself from the dangerously chaotic economic and political situation in which it found itself. The only way to deal with widespread poverty was clearly to increase production, but the administration was corrupt and the available means of transport and communication were inadequate. And, in particular, how was China to meet the outside threat, the expansionism of over-populated Japan? In his book *The Problem of China* Bertrand Russell saw very clearly that in order to save herself China would turn to military and Socialist measures, and he also realized very clearly that the wretched economic situation of the Chinese people offered favourable soil for the growth of Bolshevism. He also pointed out that the demonstrative indifference of the Chinese masses could very readily turn into burning fanaticism, and that, if it ever did, then it was likely to extend far beyond the need for solving China's own problems, in which case it would develop imperialist tendencies. Bertrand Russell quite clearly possesses an extraordinary prophetic faculty, and it is reinforced by the fact that when he looks forward his glance is not hampered by any involvement in the confused eddies of everyday politics and propaganda.

China's reaction to Bertrand Russell was equally favourable, and it was naturally strongest amongst scholars and students. At Pekin University they actually published a *Bertrand Russell Journal* in order to spread his ideas. The atmosphere he encountered in China raised his spirits, and perhaps caused him to pay too little attention to his health, for he was, after all, no longer a very young man. The fact is that he drove himself to the limit, and towards the end of his stay he went down with pneumonia, and the attack was so severe that for many days he lay between life and death in the German hospital in Pekin. The news of his sickness was cabled round the world, and Japanese newspapers actually published a report of his death. This report naturally caused alarm and dismay in Britain. A number of obituaries were actually published, and when he finally returned Bertrand Russell had the sardonic pleasure of reading them. In the meantime Chinese scholars, fearing that his death was imminent, offered to bury his body in some sacred and highly revered spot as an expression of their admiration and respect, and begged him to communicate his last message to them so that the intellectual heritage of a great man might be worthily preserved.

Fortunately this was all a little premature, and Bertrand Russell's constitution was tough enough to pull him through once more, and after a short convalescence he was able, though considerably weakened, to make the journey home, where he arrived in September 1921 after having spent about a year in China. In the meantime the *decree nisi* had been made absolute against him and he was free to marry again, which he did at once, and his secretary, Miss Dora Black, now became his wife. He had brought back various pieces of Chinese furniture and a number of Chinese carpets as souvenirs of his visit, and they were now used to furnish the house in Chelsea he was to occupy with his second wife for the next six years, during which time she was to bear him two children.

8 Books and Lectures

DURING the General Elections of 1922 and 1923 the house of the Russells was a hive of Labour activity, and Bertrand had allowed his candidature to go forward on behalf of Labour against the Conservative candidate Samuel Hoare. The constituency was traditionally a safe Conservative seat and there was little chance of winning it, but Bertrand Russell fought his campaign with great vigour and energy. In the sphere of domestic politics he called for the nationalization of the mines and the railways, and for a big increase in public spending on education, whilst in the foreign-political sphere he called for the diplomatic recognition of the Soviet Union and the rejection of the Versailles Treaty. He was defeated, of course, but his campaign won him a good deal of respect and sympathy. Nevertheless, there is very little doubt that Bertrand Russell sees too many sides to any question to make a particularly good party politician.

A recognition of this fact was probably the reason why he refused to let his name go forward as a candidate in 1924. His wife however, stepped into the breach, and in addition she did a great deal of work for other interests.

Bertrand Russell now withdrew into his study and

earned his living by his pen – indeed, he was compelled to rely more and more on this source of income. His chief interest in life was still philosophy, as it always had been, but it was his more popularly-written books and his many articles for newspapers and journals that largely provided his income. At this time he wrote regularly for *The New Leader*, a journal edited by H. N. Brailsford, who gathered such a galaxy of brilliant contributors including George Bernard Shaw, H. G. Wells, John Maynard Keynes and Julian Huxley, that the paper enjoyed a world-wide reputation. Bertrand Russell distinguished himself in this colourful if somewhat erratic gathering by his accuracy and promptitude in fulfilling his obligations, and Brailsford knew that any contribution promised by Bertrand Russell would be in his possession on time.

A further quite considerable source of Bertrand Russell's income was the fees he received for his many lecture tours in the United States.

He has never actually written a book about this country and its citizens, but his opinions can be found scattered in his other books, and in particular in *The New Leader* which published a number of articles on his American experiences. His comments extend from casual, marginal observations on the things that interest the average U.S. citizen to more profound thoughts concerning the origin and development of 'the American Way of Life'. He points out, for example, that though most Americans do not read a great deal they are zealous lecture-goers, since they seem to get far more stimulus out of seeing and meeting a great man personally than they would by reading his books.

Bertrand Russell felt that there was good excuse for this because the increasing interruption of their leisure by the tyranny of the telephone left them little time to devote to books. Generally speaking reading in the United States was a woman's hobby, and the well-situated woman felt it right and proper to her status that she should belong to a book club and read books.

Bertrand Russell has also expressed himself briefly, but to the point, on the colour question. The disparaging attitude of the average U.S. citizen towards the Negro, particularly in the Southern States, is something that Bertrand Russell can neither understand nor stomach. He was particularly struck by the outstanding role played by Jews in scientific and artistic matters and in public affairs generally, and he deplored the strong tendency towards anti-semitism he observed in the rest of the population.

He felt that the hunt for money and the status associated with it robbed the Americans of leisure, and that in consequence the average U.S. citizen was a nervous creature ridden with anxieties. One of the less desirable results of the great popularization of psychoanalysis in the United States was that the individual imposed far less restraint on his conduct than he had done before the war. In general, Bertrand Russell felt that American society was prudish and exclusive.

On the basis of his personal observations he predicted the future of the United States very accurately. He pointed out that enjoying so many and such great economic advantages would ultimately make it very powerful and that this would inevitably cause it to dominate a great part of the world. Our philosopher was unable to regard this prospect as a favourable one for the rest of the world – indeed, he was more inclined to regard it as a nightmare, and he feared that the overwhelming power of money would lead to political blackmail. Such considerations led him to recommend his own countrymen to maintain friendly relations with the United States for fear that they too might one day be victims of the finance oligarchy. He proposed in particular that Britain should accumulate large reserves of oil in order to be independent of U.S. oil monopolies. He also urged that Britain should maintain a strong navy, since the United States would respect only a strong rival. At a later date much of this seems naïve.

At this time he entertained a vague idea of some sort of international brotherhood, with the United States providing other countries with the capital they needed for their industrial development. He was firmly convinced that Socialism could be achieved only on an international scale, and he was therefore in favour of an all-embracing world organization, even if this meant the sacrifice of certain national interests.

In addition to recognizing the financial successes of the United States, Bertrand Russell also expressed appreciation of its ability to keep international relationships liberal. He foresaw that one day the United States and Soviet Russia would hold the fate of the world in their hands, and he deplored the fact that both of them concentrated far too much of their attention on utilitarian matters, and therefore had insufficient appreciation for the refinements of human civilization. He charged both countries with desiccated

Puritanism! He deplored both the domination of the amorphous mass in the United States and the domination of the dictatorial minority in Soviet Russia, which meant that philosophy necessarily came off badly in both countries, because the citizens of both worshipped at the shrine of modern technology.

Bertrand Russell's main love and interest was devoted to the natural sciences and to the philosophical problems to which man's knowledge gave rise. For example, he was on tenterhooks whilst awaiting the results of the scientific investigations into the eclipse of the sun in May 1919, which were expected to confirm Einstein's theory of relativity. By comparison with this tremendous and revolutionary advance he felt inclined to regard everything he had himself done so far as trivial.

During the busy year he was in China he nevertheless found time, in addition to all his other activities, to work out Einstein's calculations and equations, and he published his results in his book *The Analysis of Matter*, which, however, did not appear until 1927, the long delay being caused by the tremendous amount of time he had to devote to day-to-day journalism. In the meantime, however, he did publish two more popularly-written books on the same general subject: *The A.B.C. of Atoms* in 1923, and *The A.B.C. of Relativity* in 1925. He had immediately grasped the implications of the new atomic theories for theoretical physics and practical industry, and he believed that in the not all too distant future atomic energy would replace all other sources of energy in the world.

When his more profound study *The Analysis of*

F

Matter was finally published it turned out to be a strictly philosophical analysis of the effect of Einstein's theory of relativity on the age-old problem of mind and matter. His book is, in fact, the last great work on the subject to date. This new study advanced still further along the path to neutral monism which had already been laid down generally in his previous book *The Analysis of Mind*, published in 1921, and in this later book his conviction that mind and matter are subject to the same causal relations was confirmed. He supported this contention by pointing to the interacting influence of the mind, the body and the emotions in a circular continuum. Some 'events', which he describes as 'raw material', set both the logical constructions of mind and matter in movement. In his view religion was responsible for the false distinction between mind and matter, and this distinction had persisted in moralizing thought about the alleged loftiness of the spiritual and the baseness of the physical.

The philosophic ideas which resulted from his methodical analyses were summed up twenty-five years later in his book *Human Knowledge*, in which he made use of the latest results of research physics to cut the ground from underneath the old philosophical dispute about the relationship between mind and matter, and to present the whole antithesis as nonexistent and therefore not a proper subject for discussion.

9 'The School' and Moralities

IN 1927 Bertrand Russell and his extremely energetic wife, Dora, opened a school for young children in order to put his theoretical ideas on education
into practice. 'Beacon Hill School began as a joint
enterprise run by Bertrand Russell and myself', wrote
Dora Russell in 1965, describing her view of some of
the principles on which the school was conducted
under her leadership.[1]

The Russells themselves had two children of a
suitable age, and as parents they were anxious to save
them from what they regarded as the deleterious effect
of traditional education. 'We had the idea', Dora Russell continues, 'of trying to lay down some sort of basis
for a modern education, by combining what we felt to
be the best in teaching methods; in diet and care of
health; in the psychology of handling the children;
and in the subjects that we taught and the way in
which we taught them. Geoffrey Pyke and Susan
Isaacs, at the Malting House School, of roughly the
same date as ours, conducted a fundamental experiment by leaving children very great freedom, in order
to see what they would find out for themselves. We

[1] Quoted by permission from 'What Beacon Hill Stood
For' by Dora Russell, *Peace News*.

did not go so far; we did have an idea of the society into which the children would ultimately go, or rather of the society which we hoped would result from the progressive trends that were apparent and operating. . . . Our pupils were being educated to live in social systems proud of being democratic. . . . Life within the democracy was highly competitive. . . . We thought that as socialism advanced, co-operation would increase. But was a child, subject in its earliest years to parental authority – rendered all the more powerful now that families were so much smaller – likely to emerge as a self-reliant, independent-minded democrat?'

Bertrand Russell had been greatly impressed by Freud's belief that any suppression in the years of childhood could have ill effects later on in adult life, so, being a logical man, he was prepared to allow the children at his school to do whatever came into their heads in order to spare them dangerous complexes later. Whilst allowing them to do as they pleased, they also had to be instructed as to the things to avoid in later life. The idea was that they could then 'ab-react' everything perverse and sadistic in them whilst they were still young, and in this way they would get rid of all their dangerous impulses before they could harm the community. 'Freud,' says Dora Russell, 'had pointed to the distortions of personality within the family, stressing sexual frustration, Adler to the thwarting of the drive to power. Could not psychiatric findings be applied to some extent as a preventive rather than merely as a curative measure? This then, was roughly, the basis of self-government in our school. We did not deny that the child needed the background of adult protection, but held that this should express affection and a desire to help, not to inspire terror. Relief from the pressure of adult authority could be found in a community in which children lived among their equals, meeting to discuss and settle together the problems of social living as they arose day by day. Our School Council was thus not much concerned with crime and punishment; it met to discuss timetables, a bedtime rota, private versus public property in toys etc., bullying, and countless other matters which, in fact, had their counterparts in the outside world. Anyone, child or adult, could bring a complaint or a problem to the school meeting. Freedom and self-government began with our children as soon as they seemed able to take part in it, usually from about five. . . .'

It was Bertrand Russell's pacifist ideas that made him so mistrust the kind of education given in ordinary schools. In his view their insistence on obedience was deliberately pandering to the militaristic outlook demanded by the state. He felt that for anyone to risk having his head blown off in war was the height of folly, and that conventional education deliberately encouraged such stupidity. If children were brought up reasonably from the start wars would be made impossible for all time. If a child's destructive instincts were allowed to have their fling early on then, as the child became an adult, he would himself come round to the idea that the killing of human beings by human beings was the height of stupidity. Although during the course of his life Bertrand Russell himself has come round to the conclusion that state education is necessary after all, he also stresses the danger that such a system can discourage the independent teacher, and to illustrate his point he shows how after the Second World War all independence of spirit had been crushed, particularly in the teaching profession in order to cow the children and make them blindly obedient and blindly enthusiastic. Germany and Soviet Russia serve as his examples. The only way to prevent wars is to abandon narrow-minded, fanatical nationalism in favour of a common civilized ideal to be taught equally in all countries. However, he is compelled to recognize that instead of securing general acceptance this 'International Civilizatory Ideal' had lost more and more ground since the First World War.

At Beacon Hill, Dora Russell points out, 'Corporal punishment we, of course, ruled out entirely. . . . The blow of the adult hand against the child is the primary act of war. From him it passes, like a chain reaction, throughout the body politic. Proof of this came to us often in our work; as when, for instance, we were remonstrating with one of our middle group for bullying younger ones: "The Bigs tease me, so I tease the Smalls, that's fair", came the reply.'

Bertrand Russell's name and reputation were, of course, too great to allow this new educational venture to be conducted in anything but the glare of somewhat disagreeable publicity, and reporters were soon buzzing around the school and sending back ironical, mocking and highly critical accounts of life at the new school to their newspapers for the shock and diversion of the general public. A lively discussion both at home and abroad now took place about the new educational methods. The new frankness over sexual questions was criticized with particular vehemence. But, Dora Russell points out, 'Our attitude to sex education would not now be regarded with the hostility that it provoked at the time. We answered all questions about sex and the birth of babies as they arose, but had no special sex teaching. Most of our children left us before adolescence. We let them remove all their clothes in the summer if they wished to, especially for outdoor dancing and exercise.'

In the course of time Bertrand Russell himself came to the conclusion that the sexual factor did not play the enormous role in the development of children that Freud ascribed to it, and it was therefore an exaggeration to seek to account for all adult neuroses by the existence of sexual complexes from earlier years. Quite generally his views now began to diverge from those of Freud in certain questions. He declared, for example, that very often children had no desire to exercise power themselves, and were quite satisfied if they could identify themselves with their heroes, who had come to them in their reading. Provided the power urge was sublimated in this way there would be no need to fear subsequent development troubles. On the other hand, if a child had no such impulses there was a possibility that the urge would wither away, in which case the child might grow up into a resigned and indifferent adult. For this reason fairy stories with a sadistic trend were not really dangerous.

Bertrand Russell now frankly recognized that his school, as it was at present constituted, was a mistake.

Being a reasonable man he was prepared to admit that not all children were suited by the same educational methods, and, in particular, he now stressed that intellectual achievement, no matter what its character, could not be attained without discipline. He thus disengaged himself from the school and at the same time he ended his marriage. Dora Russell continued to run the school right up to 1943. The original bond of sympathy between Bertrand and Dora was that they were both unconventional in their ideas, but as their marriage developed it became clear that this very unconventionality was making its continuence pointless.

Bertrand Russell dealt with the education of children in his book *Education and the Social Order*, published in 1932. He now expressed the view that it would be wrong to send all children to the same kind of school and give them the same kind of education. Talented children, for example, would have a better chance of developing their particular talents if they were sent to special schools such as existed in France, where, in consequence, intellectual and artistic capacities were much more freely developed than in other countries. In the United States, for example, one could see that mass education resulted in a low general intellectual level. He also regarded the importance attached to the classics in traditional school education as excessive, and he proposed that the amount of time devoted to them should be reduced in favour of imparting knowledge which would really be useful to the children in later life.

This second failure did not make Bertrand Russell fight shy of marriage, and about a year later he married

Patricia Helen Spence, a young student who had assisted him in his scientific research. Patricia was known as 'Peter' to her intimates, and she frequently appears in Bertrand Russell's books under this nickname. There was one son, Conrad, of this marriage. Bertrand Russell recognized the necessity of marriage as an institution solely on account of the children. Apart from this he rejected all sexual restriction as insincere, and in particular he loathed the hypocritical sexual morality of the Victorian era, whose taboos, he felt, inevitably forced people to practise devious mental reservations. It is very likely that this loathing was responsible for many of his own excesses in the opposite direction. In particular he shocked his contemporaries by insisting that all sexual matters should be explained to children just as calmly and objectively as any other necessary information was imparted. Their natural curiosity should be fully satisfied until no secret was left. After that, he considered, they would get bored with the whole affair. Quite generally, what looked mysterious to men was only something which had not yet been sufficiently investigated. In time, however, the inquiring spirit of man would clear up all mysteries and solve all problems. These ideas and many more of the same sort are to be found in his book *Marriage and Morals*, published in 1929. Thanks perhaps to its perennially interesting subject matter this particular book sold more widely than any of his other books, though his particular treatment will have had something to do with it – the tactic of the iconoclast is to demand the impossible in the hope of obtaining the possible.

In this book Bertrand Russell sought to unmask traditional morality and to expose the falsity of those religious and moral principles which in his opinion had been the cause of a tremendous amount of avoidable misery and wretchedness in the world. He demanded equal sexual rights for women, and he regarded pre-marital sexual experience on her part not only as desirable, but, indeed, essential. He also rejected the principle of marital fidelity as out of date. Infidelity, he considered, was not a reasonable ground for dissolving a marriage, since jealousy was the most irrational feeling of all. There should be no restrictions in matters of love, since this was the sole cause of human unhappiness. Judged from the standpoint of reason alone this may have seemed logical enough, but Bertrand Russell's analysis failed to do justice to the many layers of human emotion. When, for example, did jealousy ever have anything to do with reason? Bertrand Russell's own propaganda of indifference in such matters derived from an appeal for self-control. But fundamentally such self-control is merely another form of hypocrisy and insincerity. Letting things go endangers the value of a real and devoted association based on mutual confidence, whereas precisely mutual trust and confidence make for true liberty. Reason and love represent a hostile antithesis. If instead of free love Bertrand Russell had preached renunciation in the interests of the other partner's happiness then he would have come very near indeed to the Christian ideal of brotherly love.

In all fairness it must be pointed out that apart from his more extravagant contentions some of his charges against old-fashioned moral conceptions were quite justified; and, in fact, his preachings did a great deal to break them down, and his work has certainly enlightened a good many people both at home and abroad. In particular he denounced the pharisaical treatment accorded to the unmarried mother, and the chief thing that moved him always was the desire to make humanity psychologically more healthy by striking off its chains.

One must not forget that he was speaking from the standpoint of a philosopher putting forward a new system of ethics, and that he felt he had to be ruthless in his attacks on what he regarded as deleterious. His vigorous and trenchant words have often been interpreted merely as advocacy of unrestricted sexual license, since people usually pick and choose what they care to understand. In fact his book on marriage insists very definitely that sexuality must not be regarded as a kind of hunger on the part of human nature, or become suspect as a possible source of danger; and that it is closely associated with a number of the greatest treasures of mankind.

Bertrand Russell was never mealy mouthed when discussing such matters, and so he often shocked even his friends, some of whom found it impossible to agree with him. One of these was Alfred Whitehead, with whom he had collaborated in the writing of *Principia Mathematica*. They could understand each other well enough in the scientific sphere, even though Whitehead felt it a trifle galling that Russell's name was always mentioned first in connection with their joint achievement, but this question of free love led to a breach between them. An aggravating factor was that Whitehead rather despised the popular lecture-tours Bertrand Russell carried out in the United States.

The twenties and thirties saw the deaths of many of Bertrand Russell's friends and acquaintances, and such losses moved him deeply. His letters on such occasions reveal that though little of it might show in his public attitudes he was inwardly a very sensitive man. Lady Ottoline Morrell died in 1928, and with her death the brilliant, witty and amusing gatherings which had become traditional under her roof came to an end. Unfortunately for some years before her death increasing deafness had made it impossible for her to share in the conversation, but she kept up the tradition, not wishing to deprive her friends of their pleasure.

After the first few years of Bertrand Russell's warm friendship with T. S. Eliot, the two began to find that they had less and less in common, since Eliot was now turning more and more towards the Church and away from philosophy.

The friends of former days were going different ways. Bertrand Russell and Bernard Shaw clashed because Shaw came out wholeheartedly in favour of Stalin and his régime, and refused even to consider its seamy sides. This caused Bertrand Russell to use some very harsh words, speaking bluntly of cruelty, folly and narrow-mindedness. The remarks were regarded as insulting and the breach was complete. Charles Trevelyan was another early friend who parted from Bertrand Russell on the question of Bolshevism, and by the time Bertrand married Patricia Spence two of the few old friends he had left were Robert Trevelyan and his wife.

When the Russells moved to Kidlington near Oxford Bertrand Russell gained the friendship of the biologist John Baker, and the evenings the two families spent together gave Bertrand a good deal of pleasure and interest.

In the nineteen-thirties, when he was directly dependent on what he earned with his pen, Bertrand Russell published a number of popularly-written books which, thanks to their brilliance and ingenuity, had a large circulation. For instance, there was *The Conquest of Happiness*, published in 1930, a persuasive appeal to his fellow men to search their hearts and take steps on their own account to make their lives happier and more worth while. The advice he gives in this book was based quite openly on his own experience, whose lessons he wished to see of use to all. Much the same ideas are to be found in his book *Religion and Science*, published in 1935, in which he presents life as in all probability a quite accidental occurrence, and the mind of man as, in any case, a very modest achievement of the cosmos.

In accordance with his idea that a man's personal fate and circumstances should not be allowed to govern his outlook he also interested himself in a number of other subjects of more general interest to the community, including economic theory, and in his book *In Praise of Idleness*, published in 1935, he condemns the excessive craze for saving, pointing out that money should be kept as far as possible in circulation so that everyone should have work and money to spend. The individual hoarding of money of which others were deprived was a cause of general distress. At that time this attitude was regarded by orthodox economists as standing all economic theories and ethical principles on their heads, but, in fact, it was not long (1936) before John Maynard Keynes published his book *The General Theory of Interest, Employment and Money*, in which he came to much the same conclusion.

In his book *Freedom and Organization 1814-1914*, published in 1934, Bertrand Russell analysed historical developments in Europe and the United States in that century. In particular he rejected Marx's theory that economic forces are the sole causes of historical development, and he insisted that such development was governed by economic and political theories in conjunction with the ideas of individual great men. However, the interacting relationships were so complicated that all those historians who had tried to bring any system and order into the process had constantly fallen into error. They had vainly sought to detect some scientific significance in history, but in reality there was no such significance. The book analyses the collapse of the liberal theories of the nineteenth century when they came up against the big monopolies such as those formed in the United States, and against Prussia under the leadership of Bismarck, who, instead of liberalism, had made conservatism the partner of nationalism.

Bertrand Russell felt that the biggest danger represented by any kind of state socialism would be man's never-ending urge to wield power, and he wrote a warning study in this respect entitled *Power*, which was published in 1938. In this book he insists that economic nationalism can benefit the individual only if personal liberty is at the same time guaranteed by the greatest possible measure of democracy. These problems constantly stimulated his interest in the question of how a concentration of economic power in the hands of the state could be happily reconciled with the liberty of the individual, and this then became the theme of his Reith lectures, published as *Authority and the Individual*.

10 War Years in the United States

A LL his life Bertrand Russell's chief concern was for the preservation of peace, and it was for this reason in particular that he observed the rise of Hitler and the building up of Germany's military strength with such deep anxiety. Long before war actually broke out it was clear to Bertrand Russell that a clash would come. So what attitude should his own country adopt when it did? As a pacifist he still contended that she should take no military steps whatever even to protect herself against aggression. Should the Germans invade Britain then the spectacle of a non-resisting and pacific British people would gradually convert the Germans themselves to the idea of peace, and he set out this idea in his book *Which Way to Peace?* which was published in 1936 and widely read and discussed. This time his predictions were not fulfilled and his main contentions were revealed as erroneous. His errors in this book were partly due to the fact that he was a philosopher and insufficiently conversant with the practical subject with which he was dealing, and partly to the fact that he was an enthusiastic humanist and pacifist anxious to save human civilization from a cataclysm. He assumed that a second world war must necessarily end in general chaos, and that the civilian population would be largely wiped out by chemical and bacteriological attack from the air. Such mutual slaughter would inevitably mean the end of democracy, and only a dictatorship would be able to operate in Britain on the ruins left behind by the war.

His great hope was placed in the common sense of the civilian population in his own and other countries. He hoped that they would disobey the orders of their respective governments and refuse to take part in the war. His optimism was based on the belief that the terrible experience of the first world war and its aftermath would be enough to make men hate the idea of another war so strongly that the civilian population would strike against it. But, as we know now, Bertrand Russell's estimate both of the common sense of the masses of the people, and of their ability to decide for themselves whether they would take part in a war, was grossly exaggerated. In this respect, however, he shared the illusions of most of Britain's left-wing intellectuals, who were so blinded by their ideals that they were quite unable to appreciate harsh realities. For example, British Socialist intellectuals were firmly convinced that there was an unbridgeable gulf between National Socialism and Stalinism, and that, in consequence, Stalin would never agree to co-operate in any way with Hitler. In this respect at least Bertrand Russell was not deceived, and even before the outbreak of war he prophesied that Poland would once again prove the danger point, and that, far from quarrelling over the booty, the two apparently deadly enemies would come together to share it. When the Nazi-

Soviet Pact came it deeply shocked very many people in Britain.

Although he could see very clearly how dangerous National Socialism was to world peace Bertrand Russell nevertheless greatly underestimated its misanthropic sadism. He was himself too far removed from the primitive, dogmatic lust for power which moved Hitler and his associates to realize the criminal enormities of which the man was capable. Here Bertrand Russell's deception was that of a normal, well-balanced human being incapable of conceiving of a phenomenon like Hitlerism as anything but a state of temporary madness soon to be eradicated from a free human society. It was inconceivable to him that any civilized country in the Western World could possibly fall victim to the dominance of such lunatic and criminal ideas.

Perhaps, too, his normally keen insight was blunted by the fact that here he was no longer the cool, objective scientist, and that instead he had devoted himself utterly to the cause of pacifism. Once he had adopted an idea he tended to hold on to it in all circumstances, and he would develop an enthusiasm which often led him into excess. He roundly condemned fanaticism in all its forms, but in his own way he was a fanatic himself, though it must be said that his fanaticism ended the moment his common sense brought him to recognize his error. Once he had joined a group he felt himself under a freely-accepted obligation to defend its cause; but this frequently meant that because he had surrendered his independence to a cause he was guilty of partisan errors. Whenever he still spoke as a private individual dependent on no group or party, his judgements and his prophecies were often amazingly accurate.

The world was inclined to forget that although Bertrand Russell had certainly made astonishing contributions in many spheres of human activity he was primarily a philosopher, and that in spheres outside his own he was dependent on the judgement of the experts, which meant that if they were wrong – as they so often were – he inevitably took over their errors. The respect he accorded to the judgement of the expert is evidence of his own essential modesty. This, for example, was responsible for his prediction that in the event of a second world war mankind would be largely destroyed by bacteriological warfare. This was the view of the people who were in a better position to know than others – Britain's own bacteriological warfare experts. To the horror and dismay of British Socialist friends of the Soviet Union he recommended that in the event of war between Nazi Germany and Soviet Russia Great Britain should remain neutral. His idea was to let Hitler exhaust his forces in the endless Russian steppes as Napoleon had done before him; after which the Western Powers would be able to deal with him more easily.

By this time he regarded war as a foregone conclusion, and as a pacifist he demanded that all those who did not wish to have any part in it should be allowed to leave the country. In this he was thinking not only of pacifists like himself, but also of the future of his children. The fact that he went to the United States at the beginning of the war had nothing to do with his attitude, for he went there to give a series of lectures he had undertaken. However, his stay in the United States during the war was to be a very dismal chapter in his life. The fact is that he would much sooner have been at home, sharing the dangers and privations of his fellow countrymen – particularly as the moment the shooting started his pacifism came to an abrupt end. With his usual incorruptible integrity he looked the disagreeable facts in the face and frankly admitted that there was only one way to save human civilization now and that was by the destruction of Hitler. If Hitler and his régime were allowed to survive he could see nothing but endless and terrible involvements to which human civilization must ultimately fall victim. This acknowledgement provided the world with further proof, if any were needed, of the utter sincerity of his personal character. He found it a sad, even a tragic, thing that in order to earn his bread and educate his children he had to remain away from his own country at such a time, and in this mood he would have been prepared to take up arms himself despite his already advanced age. Instead of being able to do this he had to suffer all the rigours of what one might term a cold war waged against his personal character during his stay in the United States.

He first held a course of lectures during the winter 1939-40 at the University of California, and the following autumn he was to have held a similar course at Harvard, but in the meantime he was offered a teaching appointment at the College of the City of New York to run from February 1941 to June 1942. This suited him very well, so that in order to be able to accept it, he now freed himself from his other obligations. But he had made the reckoning without his host. His ideological enemies now appeared on the scene in force and demanded that the appointment should be revoked. The first shot in the campaign against him was fired by a bishop, who declared that it was neither right nor proper that a man whose anti-religious and anti-moral attitude was notorious should be allowed to teach under public auspices in New York City. His objection was immediately reinforced by a Catholic lady who got her lawyers to file a series of charges against Bertrand Russell. The upshot of the affair was that the offer of a lectureship by the College of the City of New York had to be withdrawn.

The first thing his enemies complained of was his British nationality. Why should a doubtful character of foreign origin be given an official appointment as a lecturer in mathematics, logic and philosophy when there were plenty of suitable American citizens available to fill the post? The second point referred to a formality. The offer of an appointment had been made direct to Bertrand Russell, whereas in the ordinary way the appointment should have been publicly offered to applicants competitively. The gravamen of the objections, however, referred to his private character, his moral turpitude and his immoral preachings as a writer and lecturer. All these things, his enemies claimed, made him an altogether unsuitable person to be chosen to educate the élite of the country. The fact that he admittedly had outstanding achievements to his credit in his own sphere was adduced as an aggravating factor since there was a danger that his very brilliance might seduce his students into accepting his personal views on morality.

The offer of a teaching appointment to Bertrand Russell was condemned as in opposition to all right principles of education, and the unfortunate authorities of the College of the City of New York who were responsible had to hear themselves charged with wishing to set up 'a Chair of Indecency' at their institution. Although he was publicly placed in the pillory in this way Bertrand Russell was not given an opportunity of replying to his attackers, and the Mayor of New York at the time, La Guardia, decided that the matter would best be settled by back-stair methods. In the end, although Einstein, Whitehead and Dewey all came forward on his behalf, Bertrand Russell was not allowed to lecture in New York.

Having won this success against him in New York his enemies now thought they could repeat it in Harvard and prevent his giving the William James lectures there, but in Harvard they came up against a wall of resistance that held firm.

The whole disagreeable affair was accompanied by a spate of hostile reports in the press. Bertrand Russell's private life was dredged for material, and the unfortunate school experiment proved particularly effective against him. His situation was now that of a moral outlaw, since what had happened in New York made other education authorities chary of asking for his services, so before long the seventy-year-old found himself in difficulties in a strange land with the problem of earning his living and providing his family with money. Finally an American millionaire. Doctor Albert

Barnes, invited him to hold a series of lectures on the history of philosophy at the Barnes Foundation in Pennsylvania. A small farmhouse to the west of Philadelphia was placed at his disposal and there he moved with his family, so that for the time being his financial troubles were over. He was amiably received at the Barnes Foundation and he settled down quite happily there. Unfortunately he now fell ill, and by the time he was better again he found himself dismissed from his post. It appeared that two things had aroused displeasure: one was that Patricia Russell always appeared at his lectures wearing slacks and knitting comforts for English children, and the other that Russell's freely expressed political opinions were found offensive by Mr Barnes himself. Bertrand Russell had to go to court before he was able to obtain the money contractually due to him, and even then it was three years before it was finally paid out. In the meantime very few publications were prepared to accept articles from his pen. The United States wanted to have nothing to do with him.

Until he finally returned with his family to England he lived from hand to mouth, but fortunately for him it was only a matter of months now, and the lost sheep finally returned to the fold at the beginning of 1944. His publisher Stanley Unwin now sprang into the breach and paid him an advance on future royalties, and an American publisher also paid him an advance on a book which was to be made of the lectures he had delivered at the Barnes Foundation.

This book was *A History of Western Philosophy,* which appeared in 1945, with the sub-title 'And its

Connection with Political and Social Circumstances from the Earliest Times to the Present Day'. Whilst he was working on the book in the United States Bertrand Russell found it difficult to get hold of the works of the various philosophers dealt with. Thanks to his talent for languages he was able to read almost all of them in their original tongues. In this respect his own classical education now stood him in good stead, though only a few years previously he had been condemning the teaching of the classical tongues as superfluous items of higher education.

The result of his labour was a very thick volume which carried its readers along in a continuous line from the pre-Socratic philosophers right down to the present day. The middle of the book deals at length with the early fathers of the Church and the Scholastics. In view of Bertrand Russell's own anti-religious attitude they do not always come off well, but at least he subsequently admitted that he had learnt a great deal in his wrestling with their writings, and that in some respects he had arrived at a juster judgement on their outlook. In the preface to this book he points out that it is obviously impossible for him to know as much about each individual philosopher as can be known about him by a man whose field is narrower, and he asks the indulgence of any readers who may happen to know more than he does about this or that philosopher, pointing out that if such standards were insisted on it would never be possible to write a comprehensive history about anything. His intention was to remove the philosophers from 'the vacuum' of their individual existences and place them in the cultural and historical relationship of their own time: 'Philosophers are both results and causes. They are the result of their social circumstances and of the politics and institutions of their day. They are the cause (if they are fortunate) of convictions which help to form the politics and the institutions of subsequent periods. . . . I have done my best to present, as far as truthfulness allows, each philosopher as the result of his environment, his time and his living conditions; as a human being in whom the ideas and feelings which vaguely and intangibly imbue the human society of his time crystallize and take shape.'

In a work of this kind which attempts to review the cultural and historical relationships of philosophy it would be unfair to demand that it should deal with all the philosophers of all time, and in fact Bertrand Russell chose those who in his opinion have played the chief role in the development of man's mind. He presented philosophy as 'an essential part of the life of the community', and in so doing he created a work of a kind which had not existed before. The wealth of material presented is amazing when one considers the tremendous amount of work which was necessary to study the essential sources, and the short time in which such a vast work was written. It is a book which presents its author to us, as perhaps no other of his books does in quite the same way, as a tremendously energetic, industrious and talented writer. And the picture is all the more remarkable when you remember that this enormous labour was performed when Bertrand Russell was almost of Biblical age. Critics have pointed out errors – for example, in the chapters on Kant and

Bergson – and they have objected with some validity that the association of history and philosophy he was aiming at was not always successful. Perhaps fascinated by their philosophical ideas he had altogether neglected to place some of them in their time. Despite these objections Russell's performance is quite sufficient to assure his book a permanent place in philosophical literature.

In 1944 he was once again called to Cambridge to lecture. Because of the exigencies of the time he crossed the Atlantic in an old freighter. Opinions in England were still very divided about him, and there were influential voices at Trinity which opposed any permanent appointment. The British Broadcasting Corporation seemed somewhat hard of hearing when a proposal was made to broadcast talks by him. But on the whole he was very satisfied to be in England again and be able to lecture at his old college once more. He was now happily compensated at Cambridge for the years of hardship. The undergraduates showed their appreciation by flocking to his lectures, and although they were given in the largest available hall there were often many who could not get in. His former colleagues at Trinity received him amiably. Wittgenstein, who was then a professor of philosophy at Cambridge, was perhaps the only one really out of sympathy with Russell, but in many respects he was something of an eccentric himself.

Now and again Bertrand Russell went up to London to take part in the debates of the House of Lords. Bertrand's brother Frank had inherited the title from their grandfather Lord John Russell, and on Frank's death in 1931 Bertrand inherited the title in his turn as the third Earl Russell. He attached very little importance to it and it was seven years before he made his maiden speech in the Lords. However, in the first years after the Second World War he was often to be seen in the House of Lords.

11 Peace and Honours

BERTRAND Russell was delighted when at the General Election just after the end of the war in 1945 the Labour Party won a majority in the House of Commons and formed a government. He now hoped that a period of socialist reforms would be inaugurated in Britain to the benefit of all in a peaceful world, and his disappointment was bitter when the atom bomb was dropped on Hiroshima. He could already see the spectre of a third world war on the historical horizon, and he was well aware that it would not be long before the atom bomb was replaced by the hydrogen bomb. In the new situation he saw no alternative to the speedy rearmament of the West, which must, he felt, under all circumstances remain superior in strength to the East, since that was the only thing that could guarantee the preservation of peace. Despite all his misgivings therefore he placed himself on the side of Western Capitalism since, with all its faults, the separation of the economic and political spheres under Capitalism did guarantee greater liberty to the individual. The experience of the Second World War had taught him that a pacifist attitude alone was not sufficient to defend human liberty, and that by adopting it exclusively the world would be surrendering itself to slavery. In order to avoid this, and the victory of the dictatorships, active rearmament was now necessary for the West. Looking back, this change of mind on Bertrand Russell's part is seen to reflect changed political conditions and is easy enough to understand. But when he came forward publicly with such views after the war he had to suffer bitter attacks from the British Left, whose representatives foolishly accused him of defecting to the enemy's camp in order to curry popularity.

The British Foreign Office was now anxious to secure his services. After all, who better than this highly intelligent and articulate man to present the case for the Western World to other countries, and to convince people that the West must remain strong and united in face of the new danger? It was not long before he left on a lecture tour abroad as the ambassador of this unity. With his still inexhaustible energy he spoke in town after town and in country after country. It was very hard work, but it filled him with satisfaction, and everywhere people flocked to his meetings, which were always filled to overflowing.

His tour almost came to a sudden and tragic end in Norway in 1948. Bertrand Russell was a heavy smoker, and except when he was eating and sleeping his pipe was hardly ever out of his mouth; but smoking was forbidden in the fore cabin of the flying boat he was to take to his next destination. With his beloved pipe clenched between his teeth he took his place in the rear cabin where smoking was allowed. On the way the flying boat crashed into the sea and all the nineteen passengers in the fore cabin were drowned, while

Bertrand Russell and his fellow passengers in the rear cabin were saved—though not without suffering a ducking in the ice-cold water before they were rescued by a vessel that steamed to their aid. Bertrand Russell took this dramatic incident in his stride with his usual calm irony and he refused to indulge in any pathetic emotionalism. In clothes borrowed from the British Consul he immediately continued his lecture tour, which was devoted to constructive proposals for the avoidance of a third world war.

The general atmosphere had radically changed where Bertrand Russell was concerned and the BBC could now allow his voice to be heard on its broadcasts without incurring odium. In 1948 he was actually invited to give the annual Reith Lectures, which he did, taking as his subject the problem of authority and the individual. He recommended the nationalization of Britain's heavy industries in accordance with the programme of the Labour Party, but his primary interest was in securing the greatest possible measure of liberty for the individual. He also put forward plans for a future world government, specifying that its executive power should be largely confined to the preservation of peace, and that its existence should restrict the freedom of the individual as little as possible. This could only be ensured, he contended, if such a world State permitted its member States the greatest possible measure of autonomy, and the same principle must operate as between the individual member States.

In his old age Bertrand Russell was now numbered amongst those prominent men who had served their country well, and this status was officially confirmed in

1949 when the Order of Merit was conferred upon him. The presentation was quite an extraordinary occasion, and it was the first time that the King had conferred the highest civil order the country had to bestow on a man who had served a term of imprisonment for breaking the laws of the land, and who was, in addition, notoriously hostile to the Church of England as by law established.

In the following year Bertrand Russell's new respectable status was granted international recognition when at the age of seventy-eight he was awarded the Nobel Prize for Literature in recognition of his great services to the cause of humanity and freedom of thought.

Way back in the 'twenties Bertrand Russell took a poor view of his great contemporary Churchill, and he made one or two very disobliging remarks about him in his book *Why I am not a Christian*. Later on, and particularly during the Second World War, when Churchill's great services to his country gave Bertrand Russell cause to revise his views, the denigrating passage was removed from subsequent editions of the book.

12 Days in Australia

IN June 1950 Bertrand Russell received and accepted an invitation to visit Australia. Edward Dyason, a rich Melbourne businessman, had established a foundation for the purpose of organizing visits and lecture tours by outstanding intellectual personalities from other parts of the world. Bertrand Russell was very interested in Australia, which was the only continent he had not as yet visited, and his stay there did not disappoint him. Indeed, it was something of an event. He delivered lectures, spoke over the Australian broadcasting service, and found time to make new friendships and travel around the country. The economic and political conditions he encountered impelled him to think a good deal about the future possibilities of this new continent. He was himself essentially a European, and he envied these citizens of a very different continent their easy-going naturalness, which he found very refreshing. What he now hoped was that Australia, which was certainly prospering economically, would gradually take on something of Europe's culture and thus create an acceptable balance between the practical and the theoretical, the material and the intellectual, thus rejuvenating the ancient culture of Europe with the forthright and virile pioneering spirit of Australia. In view of the political situation – the Korean war had just broken out – Bertrand Russell urged the Australians to speed up their efforts to open up and settle their great empty spaces, as otherwise the surplus population of Asia might one day form the overwhelming majority of the population of Australia too. Because of the Korean war Bertrand Russell now greatly feared the outbreak of a third world war with wholesale destruction, and he felt that if this happened his own country would suffer more than Australia. It was at this time that he cabled urgently to London suggesting that his grandchildren should immediately be sent into the country for greater safety.

13 The H-Bomb Clash

BERTRAND RUSSELL was now quite an old man. His previous three marriages had proved failures, but at least they had left him with one happy thing – his love for and attachment to his children and grandchildren. The children of his second marriage, John and Kate, were born in 1921 and 1923 and his youngest child, his son Conrad, was born in 1937 of his marriage with Patricia Spence. In 1952 this marriage also ended with divorce. Undismayed, shortly after the *decree nisi* was made absolute, Bertrand Russell, now eighty years old, entered into a fourth marriage; this time with the lively and intelligent Edith Finch, whose family had settled in New England centuries previously. Edith had studied in Europe and she had subsequently been on the staff of Bryn Mawr. Her name first became known through her biography of Wilfred Scawen Blunt.

Despite his now very considerable age Bertrand Russell continued to interest himself closely in the political questions of the day as well as in scientific and philosophical developments, and he continued to write articles for newspapers and other publications and to give wireless and television broadcasts. His political criticism was now directed not only against the Soviet

Union, but also against the United States, and he felt that the Americans were making great mistakes in foreign policy, and that they were now suffering from the sicknesses which had afflicted England as a nascent imperialist power in the eighteenth century. The United Nations Organization was, he felt, the given forum in which the actions of the United States Government could be criticized and controlled.

Throughout his life everyday political problems had always taken up a great deal of his time and attention, but now in his old age he felt that he would like to try his hand as a writer of purely literary work. As this was completely new to him he hesitated to sign the short stories he now began to write, and the magazine *Go* published them anonymously, at the same time offering a prize of twenty-five pounds to the first reader to deduce the name of the author correctly. No one dreamed who was the author of *The Corsican Adventures of Miss X*, and the prize remained unclaimed. Bertrand Russell was much encouraged by the success of his first tentative literary attempts in the fictional sphere, and he now published a book of short stories, *Satan in the Suburbs*, written in the diction of the eighteenth century. This was then followed by a further collection of short stories entitled *Nightmares of Eminent Persons*, and this time there was obviously quite a lot of personal matter in them – Bertrand Russell found himself unable to refrain from criticizing his contemporaries once he started writing, even when, as in this case, it was supposed to be fiction.

Despite his now considerable age Bertrand Russell was not given to strict abstemiousness in living. He continued to smoke his pipe with great enjoyment and at great length, and he continued to eat just what he liked, without bothering his head about diets, though on the advice of his doctor he did transfer his allegiance from wine, which the doctor regarded as too acid for him, to whisky. As his wife also smoked they had to take turns in reading aloud, something which still gave him a great deal of pleasure, and such joint inclinations and shared pleasures did much to make their marriage agreeable and comforting. Bertrand Russell had now no illusions whatever about the world in which he lived – he knew that it was on the whole bad rather than good, and he was quite certain that there was no justice in it. But he regarded a clear-sighted understanding of the nature of the world as an essential condition for its enjoyment. To realize as soon as possible what sort of a world it was saved a great deal of disappointment and bitterness. This outlook is perhaps the secret of Bertrand Russell's own inexhaustible zest for life. Because he has always lived according to this rule of life he has been able to overcome many disappointments, and, when necessary, he has always been able to start again. Instead of wilting and feeling self-pity he has always adopted a vigorous and even aggressive attitude towards his fellow men. He is convinced that a certain measure of good, honest hatred is desirable in any man, since otherwise he would become spiritually enfeebled and himself the target for the hatred of others. This at least, was his practical attitude in life even though his theoretical beliefs often contradicted it.

In 1953 he almost died from a new attack of

pneumonia, and shortly after his recovery he had to undergo a dangerous operation. This too he survived triumphantly, thanks to his still sound constitution and his spiritual toughness.

When what he had foreseen came about, and the world was faced with the hydrogen bomb it was a matter of course for him that he should hurl his whole authority into the scales to warn mankind against this insane playing with fire. He felt that the international situation was far more dangerous in 1954 than it had been, for example, in 1950, when he had still hoped that humanity would show a little common sense. Now, with the advent of the hydrogen bomb, it really was a question of to be or not to be, and once again he entered the arena and warned all men in a passionate broadcast of the danger to the whole world of their own devilish ingenuity.

He now organized a public appeal against the hydrogen bomb to be signed by scientists all over the world. Leading personalities, both Communist and anti-Communist, rallied round him, and Einstein in particular gave him wholehearted support. It was a sad moment for Bertrand Russell when he arrived in Paris to find Einstein's written permission to use his name awaiting him as he received news of the great physicist's death. Bertrand Russell did a tremendous amount of work to make this protest document as complete as possible, and he personally visited many scientists, whilst, with the help of his wife, he wrote innumerable letters to others all over the world. He also went to Rome to deliver a speech at the Congress for World Government which was being held there. In July 1955 he arranged an important press conference, and he also appeared on television in support of his campaign. Ignoring his years and showing no consideration for his health, he did not spare himself, since he felt a personal responsibility for the fate of the world. As he had always done throughout his life he again made himself the mouthpiece of those who desired peace, stirring up the apathetic, and giving the world an example of courage and hope in his conviction as a free man that everything could still be saved. His attitude put many to shame in those days when moral and civic courage seemed at a premium, and administered a rebuke to the ostrich-like policy into which it seemed the Western World was more and more inclined to fall. The long life of this man, who was ninety years old in May 1962, has shown the world that a candid scepticism towards all traditional values need not mean a surrender to nerveless pessimism, and that a clear understanding of things and of men can be the basis for vigorous and inexhaustible optimism.

Bertrand Russell has, by example, maintained this optimistic attitude towards life. When he was sentenced in September 1961 to seven days imprisonment, because as a member of the Committee of 100 he had incited the public to stage a sit-down demonstration against nuclear armaments in defiance of police orders, he was quite undismayed, and he spent the time in his cell drafting a condemnation of the leaders of both East and West. In a letter written in April 1962 to the author of this brief sketch of his life he said that the conviction of six members of the Committee of 100 had involved him in a great deal of work, and that despite very great difficulties he was now devoting all his time to the fight against nuclear armaments. In the meantime he had not lost his old mocking humour and replying to a journalist who seemed to find it a little incongruous that a real live Lord should go in for such extreme political activities he said that he found his title quite useful because in prison at least they still treated Lords rather better than Commoners.

A life as long and as full as Bertrand Russell's is instructive and attractive the more closely you examine it, and we can look forward in particular to a film embodying his message to his fellow men. The reels are at present stored for safety in the vaults of a London bank. Altogether, the life of this 'Apostle of Humanity and Freedom of Thought' must be regarded as one long and unswerving struggle for the rights and dignity of man.

His life also demonstrates that a man who is hostile to all conventional moral and religious teachings can nevertheless harness his own moral conscience to serve the well-being of all mankind. Perhaps this is the secret of that intellectual freedom which in its own self-chosen and individual form, and with its own methods of responsible thought, turns once again to the old and constantly persisting basic values of human life. The world will not often have the good fortune to witness, in the long life of an individual outliving so many of his contemporaries, such an example of indomitable struggle. He gives, despite all the *pros* and *cons* of criticism, new courage and confidence to those in danger of losing heart and inclined to abandon the struggle to preserve human civilization. Perhaps one day the world will be less interested in Bertrand Russell's philosophical works, and in the details of his personal life, than in the splendid example of courage and human dignity he has given us. Without sentimentality or bathos we can say that men like Bertrand Russell are the real champions of humanity. When the world no longer produces his kind the freedom of man really will be in danger of extinction. Talk of heroism he wouldn't care for, so let us say then, that his personality is a striking example of a harmonious unity of conscience, word and deed.

Important Dates

IMPORTANT DATES IN THE LIFE
OF BERTRAND RUSSELL

1872   Born May 18th at Ravenscroft near Trelleck, Monmouthshire.

1874   Death of his mother.

1876   Death of his father. His grandmother, Lady Russell, takes him and his brother, Frank, to Pembroke Lodge, and supervises their upbringing and education.

1883   Appointment of a private tutor. First lessons in mathematics and philosophy. The dawn of religious doubts.

1890   Enters Trinity College, Cambridge.

1894   Attaché at the British Embassy in Paris. Return to England and marriage to Alys Pearsall Smith.

1895   Goes to Germany. Studies at Berlin University. Lectures at the London School of Economics on his return. Publication of his book *German Social Democracy*. Dissertation on the fundamentals of geometry.

1896   Visit to the United States with Alys. Mathematical lectures at Johns Hopkins University and Bryn Mawr College.

1898   Lectures at Trinity College on Leibniz. Agrees with G. E. Moore in rejecting Kant and Hegel.

1900   Attends International Philosophical Congress in Paris

1907   Active in politics. Defeated at a by-election.

1910   First volume of *Principia Mathematica* published. Lectures on mathematical logic at Trinity College.

1911   Break-up of his marriage. Criticism of Bergson's philosophy.

1914   Lectures in Boston on 'Our Knowledge of the External World.' Public speeches in England against the War.

1916   Temporary end to his academic career at Trinity College following on the Everett case.

1918   Sentenced to six months imprisonment for an article published in *Tribunal*.

1920   Visit to Soviet Russia with Labour delegation.

1921   Decree nisi made absolute. Visits China and Japan. Marries Dora Black. Birth of his son John.

1923   Second defeat at the polls, this time as Labour candidate.

1924   Lecture tour in the United States.

1927   Opening of a private school for young children together with his wife Dora.

1930   Public debate in New York with John Cowper Powys on the subject 'Is modern marriage a failure?'

1931   Becomes the third Earl Russell on the death of his brother.

1935   Divorce proceedings and the end of his marriage with Dora.

1936   Marriage with Patricia Helen Spence.

1937   Birth of his second son, Conrad.

1938   Visit to the United States. Lectures at the University of Chicago.

1939   Temporary staff appointment as lecturer in mathematics and philosophy at the University of California.

1940   His enemies secure the revocation of his appointment as staff lecturer at the College of New York City.

1941   Lectures at the Barnes Foundation in Pennsylvania on the history of philosophy.

1943   Dismissal from the Barnes Foundation.

1944   Return to England, and resumption of his academic activities at Trinity College.

1948   His plane crashes into sea off Norway where he was delivering a series of lectures on 'The Prevention of War'.

1949   Awarded the Order of Merit.

1950   Awarded the Nobel Prize for Literature. Visits Australia.

1951   Lectures at Columbia University, New York.

1952   Divorce proceedings end his marriage with Patricia. Marries Edith Finch.

1954   Collects signatures for his protest against the hydrogen bomb.

1957   UNESCO awards him the Kalinga Prize.

1960   Awarded the Danish Sonning Prize.

1961   Short term of imprisonment in connection with his appeal for a sit-down demonstration against nuclear armaments.

1962   Public speeches against nuclear armaments. Celebrations of his ninetieth birthday.